I0085611

ReCeive

God's Infinite

Love

CELESTE R. GOFF

ReCeive God's Infinite Love
Published by Celeste R. Goff

Copyright 2016 Celeste R. Goff

ISBN: 978-0-9985552-0-1

Print Edition
Printed in the United States of America

All rights reserved under international copyright law. No part of this book may be reproduced, scanned, stored in a retrieval system, distributed in any part, printed or electronic form, photocopied, recorded, or any other except for brief quotations in printed reviews, without the prior permission of the author. Please do not help or take part in piracy of the copyrighted materials in violation of the author's rights. Purchase only authorized editions.

Some names and identifying details have been changed to protect the privacy of individuals. In order to maintain their anonymity in some instances, I have changed the names and places.

Unless otherwise stated all Scripture quotations come from the King James version of the Bible.

Scriptures marked NLT® are from the Holy Bible, New Living Translation, copyright © 1996, 2004, 2015 by Tyndale House Foundation. Used by permission of Tyndale House Publishers Inc., Carol Stream, Illinois 60188. All rights reserved.

Scriptures marked NIV® are from the Holy Bible, New International Version®, NIV® Copyright ©1973, 1978, 1984, 2011 by Biblica, Inc.® Used by permission. All rights reserved worldwide.

Scriptures marked MSG are from The Message Bible Copyright © 1993, 1994, 1995, 1996, 2000, 2001, 2002 by Eugene H. Peterson Used by permission of NavPress Publishing Group.

Scriptures marked AMP are taken from The Amplified® Bible Copyright © 2015 by The Lockman Foundation, La Habra, CA 90631. All rights reserved.

Scriptures marked NASB are taken from the NEW AMERICAN STANDARD BIBLE ®, Copyright © 1960, 1962, 1963, 1968, 1971, 1972, 1973, 1975, 1977, 1995 by The Lockman Foundation. Used by permission.

Scriptures marked TLB are from The Living Bible copyright © 1971 by Tyndale House Foundation. Used by permission of Tyndale House Publishers Inc., Carol Stream, Illinois 60188. All rights reserved.

Scriptures marked GOD'S WORD® are taken from GOD'S WORD® Translation, © 1995 God's Word to the Nations. Used by permission of Baker Publishing Group.

Cover art by SIPSIDesigns
Edited by Djuana M. Daniel
10 11 12 13 — 9 8 7 6 5 4 3 2 1

Dedication

To my mother, the beautiful Evangelist Rhoda Hurt. You are my encourager who teaches me many life lessons. I gained confidence as you instilled in me how to be a professional and a woman of holiness and grace. I admire your unending hot pursuit for God which includes prayers of intercession and evangelizing. Exemplified as a co-laborer with God, I have and continue to witness countless signs, wonders and miracles for your family and so many others. It is indeed a pleasure to dedicate my book to you. I thank God for trusting you to raise me.

Love,

Celeste

Table of Contents

Foreword

Celeste Goff, who is a friend and co-laborer in the Gospel, has written a book on a topic that is near and dear to my heart and for which I share her passion. It is my pleasure to write the foreword for this in-depth writing. The author has made this book an easy-to-read, relatable book, without sacrificing true content.

With the plethora of books being written, how appropriate and necessary it is to have a book written about God's love. *ReCeive God's Infinite Love* is a book that is timely, crucial and essential for this dispensation. In this dispensation, it has been implied that to be a recipient of any true, lasting love, you must "earn" it. *ReCeive God's Infinite Love* is simple yet profound. God's love is so vast, and beyond human reasoning that many can't believe that it's as simple as receiving, and sadly for some, they never receive what has already been paid for and freely given to them by God the Father.

This age has brought in some untruths and misnomers about what true love is, how love looks, how it is attained and what is required to be a recipient of genuine love. Individuals are suffering from low self-esteem, no self-worth, and identity crisis, feeling that they are not good enough, educated enough or "pretty" enough which perpetuates them into thinking they need to "fix themselves" to "earn" or receive love.

God's love is so vast that it confused Satan and it still does; therefore, Satan attempts to confuse individuals and have them believe that

God is this tight-fisted, unreachable, never-able-to-please God, who is too good or Holy to love you because you haven't been good enough. To the contrary, God's grace (which is His love) and mercy are always extended not being based on performance. What Satan doesn't want you to know is how much God really does love you. He so loved us that although the earth realm was not conducive to receive God's sovereignty, holiness, and glory, God, who loved the man He created so much, found a way to send Himself to us through His Son, Jesus the Christ, incarnate, to reconcile His man back to Himself. He said, "…and they shall call his name Emmanuel, which being interpreted, is God with us" (Matthew 1:23). Even after gross sin and man's continued disobedience, God's love for us transcended space and time, and His mercy and love continued to pursue us. Hallelujah for His love.

In this book, ReCeive God's Infinite Love, Celeste's exegesis of the infallible Word of God gives an exhaustive list of scripture references. I enjoyed the true-life stories that resulted in victorious outcomes that demonstrate, for the skeptic, God's love in action. I invite you to read ReCeive God's Infinite Love and gift the book to someone who may be struggling in this area. This book has the potential to change the very course of an individual's life and can be instrumental in setting one on a path of knowledge. For knowledge is power, and many are destroyed, the Bible says, for the lack of knowledge.

Readers can expect to receive instruction, encouragement, compassion, sympathy, a call to action and understanding. Celeste will take you on a wonderful journey of exploring the possibilities of experiencing this love. You will feel the compassion and the desire she has for you to experience the unending love of God that we mutually experience.

The author shares an in-depth explanation of Ephesians 3:17-18, a scripture that I frequently preach, quote, share and encourage others with. I believe this scripture is the essence of this book. It is a prayer that I pray for each reader...that you will know and receive "what *is* the breadth, and length, and depth, and height" of God's Infinite Love.

Pastor Betty Evans
Kingdom Life Christian Center, Chicago, IL.

Acknowledgments

Giving honor to whom it is due is very important to me:

My Savior and Lord Jesus Christ who changed my life forever; If it hadn't been for you, I would not be able to write this life-changing book of your infinite love. Much fruit shall be produced.

To my family who is the fabric of our heritage; Your support is weaved into my DNA.

Dr. Bill Winston, my pastor who is the epitome of a man of faith and God's power. Your teaching and preaching the Word of the God with the desire and heart to see people excel in fulfilling our highest calling trusting only in God is admirable. Your anointing for Kings and Priests is uniquely preeminent and life-transforming. My children and I are impacted by you and are increasing more and more.

Dr. Cindy Trimm, you are a highly influential and empowering leader of God's choice in my life. As a bestselling author, your powerful books, teachings and empowerment sessions have changed the trajectory of my life for expansion. Your advice was invaluable to me in completing my first book. As I always tell you, "You are God's gift to humanity!" I am honored to say you are my mentor and friend.

To my friend, Dr. Tanesha House thank you for your continual prayers, support and keeping me accountable with the writing of my book.

Introduction

ReCeive God's Infinite Love

This book was birthed in my spirit by God's still small voice in 2009. I want to share a little bit about the specific situation that inspired me to write it. I have a friend, who I will call Keisha, who shared with me some very painful times she experienced in her life through emotional and verbal abuse from her husband. On one pivotal evening, she ran into the bathroom, her face stained with tears, eyes swollen and bloodshot. My heart went out to her, and I was deeply moved in my spirit. I had prayed with her for many years. But this time was different.

I heard the Lord say, "Write a book about My love." At that moment, I paused, and God's love just poured over me like warm honey. He impressed upon me that His love surpasses everyone's understanding, and is exemplified every day without fail. I had never written a book nor had I ever desired to write one. However, in obedience to God and with an anticipation that this act would help many others who wanted real everlasting love, I said "yes" to God.

I had known my friend for decades. She had experienced challenges her entire marriage being a unique individual. She struggled with abuse in the form of control, manipulations and mind games. She was also spiritually abused, which is when someone harasses another person by use of coercion or persuasion to impose their erroneous religious beliefs to proselytize a person. There was always a battle between the kingdom of darkness and the kingdom of light. My heart went out to her as I prayed and would recommend that they go to counseling. However, to no avail, her narcissistic husband refused to go, stating that nothing was wrong. She suffered not able to fully realize her own destiny and identity. All of that accompanied by emotional pain, fear and rejection. She was hopeful yet fearful. Fear overshadowed every decision as she wasn't sure what would set off an angry rage in her spouse. She always experienced a challenge in their marriage to keep a peaceful atmosphere in their home. Her personality became suppressed and smothered. As a believer in Christ, her husband treated her as "the enemy."

However, she always expressed to me that she desired a loving marriage and partnership to raise their children. I shared with her God's Word in Amos 3:3, which states, "How can two walk together, except they be agreed?"

She was in a marriage yet existing like a lonely, single individual. The night prior to the marriage ceremony, she said the Holy Spirit told her not to go through with the marriage.

Singles, please marry for the right reasons. Most importantly, I want to caution you to hear and follow God's direction for the mate He has designed for you. My friend is the type of person who prefers things be in order and did not seek God's counsel. She had gotten pregnant before marriage and was trying to patch things on her own. Her intentions were good, but not expedient.

2

Proverbs 14:12 states, "There is a way which seems right unto an individual, but the end thereof *are* the ways of death." Her marriage ended in "death" or divorce. After years of seeking an answer of what to do, she finally got a release and the courage to file for divorce. Thank God that their children have the reverential fear and admonition of the Lord. The children have survived this experience by knowing the God of Truth, which ultimately spared them the confusion of witnessing their parents in an unhappy marriage. She persevered in raising her children in the admonition of Proverbs 22:6 to train your children in the way they should go and when they are old, they will not depart.

Now, fast-forward to 2015. I attended a tent church service in my hometown where the guest speaker was a prophet. He was operating under the unction of the Holy Ghost with a "word of wisdom and knowledge," and he turned to me during the service and said, "Finish that book you are writing, because it will bless others." This prophet did not know me or anything about me. Only two people were aware that I was writing a book. I was astonished and elated because I knew it was God speaking directly to me. I had procrastinated and did not write for several years. I praised God for the encouragement to finish the book, and I began to write again.

A few months following the tent church service, I received another confirmation during a prayer conference call. Usually, five to six people are on the call, but on this particular day, it was only two of us. My fellow prayer intercessor on the phone asked if I had any special prayer requests. I replied, "No I do not" because we usually have a prayer topic

3

and take special prayer requests. She was led by the Holy Spirit to pray for me. She began to pray for my family and me, and lastly in regards to my book! I barely knew her name, as we never met in person. Our group gathered only on the phone to pray. I did not tell her I was writing this book. She prayed mightily regarding resources needed for this book. I am always astonished at God's goodness and faithfulness. As the scripture reads in 2 Corinthians 13:1 "...out of the mouth of two or three witnesses let every word be established." The mandate to complete the book was still in force.

This book, ReCeive God's Infinite Love, cannot adequately define our Creator, who is God, the Almighty Self-sufficient One's, supreme love. You can only find God's love in the context of his Holy Word which you cannot annul and in your personal experiences. God's love demonstrated is inconclusive and inexhaustible. It is exemplified every day when we awaken to see a new day filled with His new mercies. As I have received revelation of God's love toward us, I have shared that revelation with you. This book is not a religious book and truthfully speaking, God is not religious—God is love (1 John 4:7-12). He is Creator and sustainer of every living thing, and we are His most prized possession. We understand and recognize that there are many great inventions in the world today. Sometimes we do not take the time to research who the inventors are, but we enjoy their creativity. I recommend that you take the time to study the Holy Bible to explore our Creator's mindset and best desire for us.

As God's most valuable creation, our heart's desire should be to comprehend His unfailing love for us! Paul the Apostle prayed:

That Christ may dwell in your hearts by faith; that ye, being rooted and grounded in love, may be able to comprehend with all saints what is the breadth, and length, and depth, and height; And to know the love of Christ, which passeth knowledge, that ye might be filled with all the fulness of God.

Ephesians 3:17-19

The dimensions of God's love in this scripture are similar to that of roots of a plant or tree; they are measured as breadth, length, depth, and height. Just picture a plant's roots in the ground—they go down deep, are long, and they grow wide. Dimensions are realized only when stretched in those directions.

Therefore, as with an individual, if they are stagnant in life, they will not have the adventure of experiencing the dimensions of God's love. When you realize that God loves you and is your supporter you can move forward and be confident that nothing shall be impossible for you according to His will and tailor-made purpose for you. To know His love, which passes knowledge is to know Him intimately. Intimacy is experienced only in a relationship. "Passing knowledge" means it goes well beyond or supersedes anything that you can intelligently imagine. Wow, that is amazing! This is how far-reaching His love is toward us. We have the potential to be filled with the fullness of God's love.

Paul's prayer is that we would understand the revelation of God's love through Jesus Christ by these measurements: The breadth exemplifies love's extent to all nations. The length is never ending because as far as the East is from the West, the Bible says they never meet. By the way, this is also how far He has removed our transgressions. Psalms 103:12 says, "As far as the east is from the west, so far hath he removed our transgressions from us." The depth is His saving grace to all no matter how low you have fallen or how deep you have sunken into despair. The height refers to us being raised up and seated with Jesus Christ.

The universe is replete with the essence of God's love. *Essence* is defined as, "the intrinsic nature or indispensable quality of something, especially something abstract, that determines its character."[1] Since God is love, His essence permeates everything. That means every organism is sustained by God.

Agape is an ancient Greek word, which means love.[2] It is the highest kind of love. It only comes from God's exemplary love. He is the originator. We have seen it expressed throughout all generations. Even now, we are experiencing it. Just look around you. Are you reading this book in the spring, summer, fall or winter? Peer out of the window. Do you see trees budding or flowers blooming? How about the smell of fresh cut grass? After it is cut, more is replenished. Possibly, it could be wintertime and nature is resting. During the fall season, plants take on an array of colors. Other examples include the purpose of the constellation, the moon, sun, and other planets. They all have a part to play for the upkeep of the universe. According to Romans 1:20 NLT:

> For ever since the world was created, people have seen the earth and sky. Through everything God made, they can clearly see his invisible qualities—his eternal power and divine nature. So they have no

excuse for not knowing God.

Now for the best of all, get a mirror and look at the person's reflection in it. Wow, look at you! Did you know that you are made in the image and likeness of Almighty God? (Genesis 1:26) God created you just like Him.

What is love? Love is an expression, a demonstration, and a manifestation. Expression calls for an action. Demonstration is proof. Manifestation is materialization. Love is never dormant. As an expression, demonstration, and manifestation of His love, God gives out from Himself which is love.

I pray that after reading this book, you are ready to receive God's love.

Father, I thank you that the individual reading this book will receive your revelation knowledge that will flow freely and uninterrupted. Also, that their spirit may be enlightened, so that they will know the hope of your calling, and the riches of your glorious inheritance. Will you will speak to their hearts by your Holy Spirit so that their lives will never be the same, but changed for proper divine alignment? Lord, be glorified and exalted in Jesus Christ Name, Amen.

Let's have God's Love Encounter!

Chapter One

The Constitution of Man

What are mere mortals that you should think about them, human beings that you should care for them? Yet you made them only a little lower than God and crowned them with glory and honor. You gave them charge of everything you made, putting all things under their authority.

Psalm 8:4-6 NLT

God is perfect, and He loves us so much. Now, this may come as a surprise to you but you are perfect too. That is, in your regenerated spirit. In other words, you are "regenerated" or re-*gened* by being born of the Spirit of God. Your spirit is new not your physical, human body or genes which comprise your functional heredity.

We are tri-part beings with a spirit, a physical body and a soul. God desires that you receive His love in the totality of your being—spirit, soul and body. Throughout this book, I will share my testimonies of how I am and continue to be a recipient of God's love.

OUR SPIRIT

In the book of Genesis, God formed man out of the dust of the ground then breathed life into his spirit which is the core of our existence as a person. However, in the earth realm, our spirit is invisible to

9

the physical eyes. We have an "earth suit" which is our body in order to function on this terra firma. It is our personification or embodiment that people cannot visualize with their physical eyes. The Word of God states that man was created in the image and likeness of Him, which is our spirit. Our spirit is that which becomes born again. The Holy Spirit makes His abode in us within our spirit.

> God spoke: "Let us make human beings in our image, make the reflecting our nature So they can be responsible for the fish in the sea, the birds in the air, the cattle, And, yes, Earth itself, and every animal that moves on the face of Earth." God created human beings; he created them godlike, Reflecting God's nature. He created them male and female. God blessed them: "Prosper! Reproduce! Fill Earth! Take charge! Be responsible for fish in the sea and birds in the air, for every living thing that moves on the face of Earth."
>
> Genesis 1:26–28 MSG

Thinking back to the time when I received the gift of the Holy Spirit, I was a little girl at the tender age of 11. According to the book of Acts in chapter two, I asked the Lord for the Holy Spirit to make His abode in me and received this precious gift with the evidence of speaking in other tongues. It was a great day. Following the Sunday morning service that I attended, I was taken to what was referred to as the "Power Room." This is where people would go to "tarry" or wait to receive this gift. When a person tarries, they often repeatedly say, "Thank you, Jesus," "Glory to God," or "Hallelujah" until their language changed to whatever the Holy

Spirit wanted to say through them. A person would just yield their speech and heart to the Lord, and allow Him to infill them with the Holy Spirit. This is not something that a person can "work up." It takes a heart that is open to God, ask Him and just receive His gift. Luke 11:13 says,

> If ye then, being evil, know how to give good gifts unto your children: How much more shall *your* heavenly Father give the Holy Spirit to them that ask him?

Once I was in the room, I knelt on my knees, put my face in the corner of the pew and began to thank the Lord over and over again. The next thing I knew, my language had changed, and I was speaking in other tongues as the Holy Spirit gave me utterance. I could not stop, as I was overwhelmed with power and jubilance. The customary practice for the ministry workers was to identify those who were speaking in tongues, bring them to the front of the church so that they could tell everyone their name, and give a testimony of their experience. The workers discovered me on my knees and brought me to the front, while I was still yet speaking in tongues. I was "drunk" in the Spirit as on the Day of Pentecost in Acts 2. I was not able to tell them my name immediately because of what I was experiencing. The leader told everyone, "She got the Holy Spirit the old fashion way." I believe she was referencing the account on the Day of Pentecost when 120 people gathered in the Upper Room were perceived as "drunk." The baptism of the Holy Spirit as recorded in the book of Acts is still relevant today.

And when the day of Pentecost was fully come, they were all with one accord in one place. And suddenly there came a sound from heaven as of a rushing mighty wind, and it filled all the house where they were sitting. And there appeared unto them cloven tongues like as of fire, and it sat upon each of them. And they were all filled with the Holy Ghost, and began to speak with other tongues, as the Spirit gave them utterance. And there were dwelling at Jerusalem Jews, devout men, out of every nation under heaven. Now when this was noised abroad, the multitude came together, and were confounded, because that every man heard them speak in his own language. And they were all amazed and marvelled, saying one to another, Behold, are not all these which speak Galilaeans? And how hear we every man in our own tongue, wherein we were born? Parthians, and Medes, and Elamites, and the dwellers in Mesopotamia, and in Judaea, and Cappadocia, in Pontus, and Asia, Phrygia, and Pamphylia, in Egypt, and in the parts of Libya about Cyrene, and strangers of Rome, Jews and proselytes, Cretes and Arabians, we do hear them speak in our tongues the wonderful works of God. And they were all amazed, and were in doubt, saying one to another, What meaneth this? Others mocking said, These men are full of new wine. But Peter, standing up with the eleven, lifted up his voice, and said unto them, Ye men of Judaea, and all ye that dwell at Jerusalem, be this known unto you, and hearken to my words: For these are not drunken, as ye suppose, seeing it is *but* the third hour of the day. But this is that which was spoken by the prophet Joel; And it shall come to pass in the last days, saith God, I will pour out of my Spirit upon all flesh: and your sons and your daughters shall prophesy, and your young men shall see visions, and your old men shall dream dreams: And on my servants and on my handmaidens, I will pour out in those days of my Spirit; and they shall prophesy:

Acts 2:1-18

OUR SOUL

Our soul is our mental state of various behaviors and mannerisms. It is the way we conduct ourselves in reaction to circumstances and situations. Our soul consists of our mind, will, emotions and intellect. It is highly important for our souls to be healthy because it is in our mind or the human's central processing unit where we make life decisions, and where reasoning occurs. The Bible tells us to renew continually our mind in order to live a fulfilling life. Everything that we need pertaining to life and godliness is in the Word of God. The renewing of our mind happens when we use His Word as our plumb line of divine standard for life's choices. Like Prego® pasta sauce advertises, "It's in there."

And be not conformed to this world: but be ye transformed by the renewing of your mind, that ye may prove what *is* that good, and acceptable, and perfect, will of God.

Romans 12:2

It is God's desire that our totality is in alignment

with His will, plan and purpose for our lives. Just think, it is impossible to depart from your home, leave your spirit there, and arrive at your destination in "totality." Hence, we are the sum total of who the Lord has created us to be. Scripture clearly states that we are tri-part beings in 1 Thessalonians 5:23,

> And the very God of peace sanctify you wholly; and *I pray God* your whole spirit and soul and body be preserved blameless unto the coming of our Lord Jesus.

We cannot receive God's love until we hear the good news, process it in our mind as His Holy Spirit reveals it to our spirit, and we subsequently embrace and receive His love. The challenge for a person receiving God's love comes when our mind (our soul) is presented with this truth, and we attempt mentally to comprehend His love. Sometimes an embedded negative thought pattern or fear prevents us from receiving the love of God. What we must realize is that the revelation of God's love is never hidden from us; it is hidden for us. I encourage you just to receive God's love as He wraps His arms around you. Once you are ready to receive Him, He reveals His love to you. Some may feel that God's love inconceivable and ask why God Almighty the Sovereign One loves us unconditionally despite ourselves. Some may even have an overwhelming sense of guilt and condemnation. I want to encourage you not to be discouraged. Jesus Christ said,

> For God sent not his Son into the world to condemn the world; but that the world through him might be saved.
>
> John 3:17

He loves us just as we are. It does not matter

14

where you have been or your current status in life. Society may have overlooked you. Others may not value you, but God sees you as highly valued and "loveable" (smile). So much so, that He sacrificed His Son to die for you and everyone else—the entire world. Jesus conquered death, so that we may live righteously and be in right standing with God. This is achieved only by accepting Jesus Christ as Lord.

I remember when I experienced a panic attack. It happened all of sudden, out of nowhere and it originated in my soulish realm, the mind. An overwhelming feeling of unexplainable fear engulfed and consumed me. I felt like I was going to die. I was confused and overtaken sensing I was separating from reality. I felt anxious and helpless. I contacted my doctor about the occurrence, and she prescribed an anti-depressant. I had the prescription filled and took one pill that evening. The effect of that one pill caused my body and mind to be listless and lethargic. It was horrible. I felt that I was not in control, lifeless, and in an almost incoherent state of mind. When I regained normalcy, I refused to take another pill. I could not imagine how I could drive or even work in that condition.

Then another panic attack hit me mid-morning while sitting at my desk at work. Immediately, I got up from my desk, hurried to the lunchroom, and paced the floor. I did not know what to do. The Holy Spirit impressed upon me to begin praising and worshipping the Lord. No one was in the lunchroom at the time. I lifted my hands in the air and began to praise and worship God. Guess what! The heaviness immediately lifted. A divine supernatural peace and quietness came upon me. One moment in the presence of God can change everything! I am now free from the dark spirits of panic attacks that attempted to overtake me. Even today those spirits are attacking people everywhere.

Currently, the market is flooded with anti-depressants and anti-anxiety medicines prescribed to the masses. The purpose of these medicines is to treat and not cure the ailment. My experience, as well as others, was a robotic state of mind unable to function with freedom of thought and expression. God has not designed us to live this way. The enemy comes to steal our peace and wholeness. We should not allow his devices to affect our well-being. He is out to deceive God's creation and detach us from what is rightfully ours, which is a right relationship with God. God loves us too much to leave us. He meets us where we are. Glory to God!

Our soul is the connector to our spirit and body; it is our "decider" or "chooser." Will you decide to prosper or be impoverished? Will you choose to worship in spirit and truth or not to worship? It is crucial that we allow our spirit to be directed by the Holy Spirit. This will enable us to make beneficial choices, and subsequently, our body will submit and follow. Our body does nothing of itself. It is a slave. Without our spirit, the body cannot function.

When we fast from food, we deny our body food. This enables us to hear God more clearly in our spirit. Our spirit becomes more sensitive, and we exercise more authority over our body and mind. Whatever you nourish the most will become stronger. Have you ever fasted and your body seemed like it whined for food? Some people call it hunger pangs. I've had to tell my body very sternly,

"Be quiet, you're not getting any food today!" I had to keep my body as a slave as it says in 1 Corinthians 9:27 NASB, "But I discipline my body and make it my slave, so that, after I have preached to others, I myself will not be disqualified." Another benefit of fasting is that we can think with more clarity. Our choices and decisions are more in alignment with the voice of the Good Shepherd, Jesus Christ (John 10:14, 27). Our mind signals our brain, which is connected to our spinal cord which has nerve impulses for bodily movement. The enemy's desire is to ensnare our mind; this is where decisions originate, and subsequently, our body follows.

When we are not fasting, more time is consumed thinking about what we will eat, then we shop for the food, prepare the meal, and ultimately eat the meal. All this time spent can be redirected to God by reading His word, praying and meditating.

As a comparison of the inseparable framework of mankind, when we receive Jesus Christ, we receive God Himself and the Holy Spirit. Everything God has purposed to do has already been done through His Word. God cannot be separated from His Word. They are one (John 1:1). God does not waste His words. Whatever He says comes to pass. In the book of Hebrews, a profound truth and mystery are revealed.

> The Son is the radiance of God's glory and the exact representation of his being, sustaining all things by his powerful word. After he had provided purification for sins, he sat down at the right hand of the Majesty in heaven.
>
> Hebrews 1:3 NIV

For He has rescued us *and* has drawn us to Himself from the dominion of darkness, and has transferred us to the kingdom of His beloved Son, in whom we have redemption [because of His sacrifice, resulting in] the forgiveness of our sins [and the cancellation of sins' penalty]. He is the exact living image [the essential manifestation] of the unseen God [the visible representation of the invisible], the firstborn [the preeminent one, the sovereign, and the originator] of all creation. For by Him all things were created in heaven and on earth, [things] visible and invisible, whether thrones or dominions or rulers or authorities; all things were created *and* exist through Him [that is, by His activity] and for Him. And He Himself existed *and* is before all things, and in Him all things hold together. [His is the controlling, cohesive force of the universe.]

Colossians 1:13-17 AMP

Only through Jesus Christ—then and only then—will we perceive God's love and receive His overwhelmingly great love toward us. Ignorance is our greatest enemy to this profound truth. Ignorance is not stupidity; it is unawareness.

OUR BODY

God formed our physical bodies directly from the ground. It is comprised of the material that gives us the ability to function in the visible atmosphere as described:

And the LORD God formed man *of* the dust of the ground, and breathed into his

nostrils the breath of life; and man became
a living soul.

Genesis 2:7

You may or may not be satisfied with your body. Some people may say, "I'm too fat, I am too skinny, or I have blemishes, etc." As a side note, may I dare ask who sets the standard of excellence for our physiology? Who and what dictates the appropriate standard? That is something to consider. However, it is important to keep our body fit and give it the proper nutrients to defend against disease.

Anatomically, God has designed the body to heal itself. Our body's system consisting of cells, tissues, and organs work in tandem to keep us functioning. Most times, medications hinder this process. This is why numerous side effects accompany prescription drugs.

We do not have to rely on these man-made medications to heal our bodies. God healed me holistically by instructing me on the proper foods to eat. As an added bonus, I lost twenty-five pounds within three months. I had been praying and believing God for years to lose that exact amount of weight. I did not know how it would happen because dieting and other methods were unsuccessful. But "as for God, His way is perfect" (Psalm 18:30).

I was on prescribed pills for ten years to relieve acid reflux, heartburn, and indigestion. While on the medication, I was able to eat anything I desired. However, I noticed that when I missed two consecutive days of taking it, the symptoms would come back with a vengeance. Consequently, I would experience uncomfortable days and sleepless nights. Then I cried out to God and said,

"Lord, something is not right. I will not be on this medication for the rest of my life." My body was accustomed to and dependent on the medication to eat and sleep comfortably. It was imperative for me to address the root of the problem.

God directed me to research natural remedies found in foods. I began to add fermented foods, live cultures, and alkaline water to my diet. However, sweets were the hardest to let go! Since sugar intensified the adverse effects I experienced, I eliminated all sugary treats. I also considerably reduced my intake of meats and seafood because they are highly acidic. My digestive system was healed by incorporating foods in my diet that were advantageous for a healthy lifestyle. I now have more energy that I had not experienced in decades. God has made us wonderfully intricate. Let's take care of our body; we only have one!

Chapter Two

Foolishness to Man is Wisdom to God

For the message of the cross is foolishness [absurd and illogical] to those who are perishing and spiritually dead [because they reject it], but to us who are being saved [by God's grace] it is [the manifestation of] the power of God. For it is written and forever remains written, "I WILL DESTROY THE WISDOM OF THE WISE [the philosophy of the philosopher], AND THE CLEVERNESS OF THE CLEVER [who do not know Me] I WILL NULLIFY."

1 Corinthians 1:18–19 AMP

Do you know of anyone who would come to earth, and live life as man and experience life as we know it and purposefully die? Almighty God experienced life as well as death for everyone through the person of Jesus Christ. God wrapped Himself in flesh according to John's writing:

> And the Word was made flesh, and dwelt among us, (and we beheld his glory, the glory as of the only begotten of the Father,) full of grace and truth.

John 1:14

God's ultimate plan for mankind is to love us. We were ransomed from the imprisonment of Satan by the precious, guiltless blood of Jesus Christ. What a great sacrifice He paid! God then reconciled us to Himself through the blood of Jesus Christ. Reconciliation is the process of getting back into proper relationship with someone. God loves us so much that even before we were born, He laid down His life for us. God came from above in the form of man to rescue us. The personification of God's love is shown through Christ Jesus, who is Savior, Lord, and Redeemer. You may say, "God does not know what I am going through!" I have to differ with you. He knows everything about you. Even the hairs on your head are numbered by Him (Luke 12:7). That means that each hair on your head has a number associated with it. God came to earth to experience life as a human legally through the birth of a virgin, Mary (Matthew 1:21–23) in the person of Jesus Christ who is our High Priest. Therefore, He can identify with us. Hebrews 4:15 tells us,

> For we have not an high priest which cannot be touched with the feeling of our infirmities but was in all points tempted like as *we are*, *yet* without sin.

The fulfillment of God's plan of love is Jesus' life, which was sacrificed on the cross. His sacrifice paid the price, once and for all for everyone (Hebrews 10). He made restitution for our sins without guilt and without sin and restored our ability to have a relationship with God. And guess what? We do not have to qualify for His eternal love. While we were doing "our thing," He had us in mind. As I mentioned earlier, it may seem weak and foolish to the natural human mind. It was His eternal love that baffled the kingdom of darkness. If the evil spirits knew that when Jesus Christ was crucified on the cross that all people would be made free from Adam's transgression, they would not have fallen into God's wondrous epic plan. It is through God's divine wisdom that everyone can be saved.

> But we speak the wisdom of God in a mystery, *even* the hidden *wisdom*, which God ordained before the world unto our glory: Which none of the princes of this world knew: for had they known *it*, they would not have crucified the Lord of glory.
>
> 1 Corinthians 2:7–8

By God's design, He leads and guides us through our spirit. Have you ever heard anyone say, "Oh, my mind is playing tricks on me?" One can be easily misled by what they see with their physical eyes and hear with their natural ears especially if they are not connected with God. One prime example is the media. The media can have an emotional rollercoaster effect on its viewers and hearers. We must learn to recognize and rely on God's voice and obey Him. How can we do this? It is by having faith in what He is leading us through and to, which is only for our good not to harm us.

God has mysteries that are hidden in plain sight in the realm of the spirit. At the appointed time, the light of God reveals His truth and those things prepared for His children. He has the answer to every question we may present to Him. However, the wisdom of God has its protocol. You cannot gain His wisdom and insight without first receiving Jesus Christ as Savior and Lord. If you are not born again, when you read the Holy Bible, which is the Kingdom of God's constitution for His children, you cannot fully comprehend His constitution.

All rights, laws, benefits and power lies within every country's constitution. When you are born again, you are born of the Kingdom of Heaven, which is ruled and reigned by God Himself. Perhaps in another book, I will write about the Kingdom of God and His royal family, but in the book of John, chapter three, Jesus Christ explains that to see or "understand" the Kingdom of God, you must be born again. Oh, such love.

ANOTHER DIMENSION

As a young adult, I had an out of body experience where I believe I was in heaven. There is no doubt in my mind at all. I will never ever forget this experience. I don't know whether I had died or not. I went to bed one night, and after I had fallen asleep, this is what happened. The next thing I knew, I entered another dimension where the atmosphere was absolutely perfect and extremely peaceful. I thought to myself; I'm in heaven. The dimension I had entered was so bright with light. The light was like a living organism which filled the place. The brightness was not uncomfortable for my vision. I was in awe of just being in that dimension. It was like I was in unison with the atmosphere of heaven. I was looking around and could sense the presence of the Almighty God. His love permeated the place. All I experienced was pure goodness. The expression on my face was a contented smile. I was elated to be there coupled with utter amazement. As I was thoroughly enjoying myself in that dimension, all of a sudden I found myself back in my bed. The speed was faster than immediate. A family member had entered my bedroom and brushed against my feet at the foot of the bed.

When I felt the brush, it caused me to return to this dimension where the room was dark. Heaven is in another dimension. It is more real than this temporal life we are living on earth. (2 Corinthians 4:18)

Chapter Three

God's Infinite Love

For God so loved the world, that he gave his only begotten Son, that whosoever believeth in him should not perish, but have everlasting life. John 3:16

The word *world* in the scripture referenced above is translated from the Greek as "kosmos."[3] God created the universe, everything and everyone in it. It is His divine order and congruous arrangement. Additional biblical and Greek usages of this word from *Thayer's Greek Lexicon* are:

- an apt and harmonious arrangement or constitution, order, government

- ornament, decoration, adornment, i.e. the arrangement of the stars, 'the heavenly hosts,' as the ornament of the heavens. 1 Peter 3:3

- the world, the universe

- the circle of the earth, the earth

- the inhabitants of the earth, men, the human family

- the ungodly multitude; the whole mass of men alienated from God, and therefore hostile to the cause of Christ

- world affairs, the aggregate of things earthly[4]

God's infinite love is "giving." Several synonyms for the verb "giving" are: contributing, conveying, dispensing, distributing, endowing, granting, imparting, presenting, remitting, supplying, and transferring.

God gives, and gives, and gives. To give means "to freely transfer the possession of something to someone; hand over to."[5] According to Dr. Cindy Trimm, "Certainly, this is the greatest expression of love ever. This kind of love is not based on feelings; it is a decision that requires sacrifice. Love is your commitment to the people important to you; it is unselfishly giving up what you have for the benefit of someone else."[6] God is not selfish; He does not discriminate. He loved the world and gave His only begotten Son. His creation is the best; therefore, God gave us His best.

Sample References of God's Giving Characteristics of Love:

A New Heart	Ezekiel 36:26
Sun and Rain	Matthew 5:45
Gives Us Authority	Luke 10:19
Water	John 4
Bread and Water	John 6:35, 51
Abundant Life to Us	John 10:10b
Peace	John 14:27
Jesus Gave His Life	John 10:17–18; Galatians 1:4
Holy Spirit	John 14:15–18; Romans 5:5
Gives Us Power to Witness	Acts 1:8
The Measure of Faith	Romans 12:3

Richly All We Need for Enjoyment	1 Timothy 6:7

God does not direct his love to any particular group of people. He loves and desires to have a relationship and live through everyone, His creation. Genesis 11 says He is God over every nation. God is ready to daily direct us so that we can have a wonder-filled and adventurous life.

God's love is not earned. He does not operate on a merit-based system with unattainable requirements. Because some people believe that they must qualify, they become hopeless thinking God has turned His back on them. But that is contrary to God's nature. This type of thinking stems from the root of fear where some feel that they will not be accepted. When people have not had an experience with the genuine agape love of God, what develops is a negative self-defeatist mindset. Some may go as far as to say, "God does not love me, He is waiting to punish me for what I have done, and continue to do." This is a tactic and trick the devil uses to bring shame and keep people trapped in unfruitful emotions of unworthiness and separated from God's fulfilling, abundant love.

Remember, God's love is perfect. The word *love* translated from the Greek language is "agape."[7] *Thayer's Greek Lexicon* defines *agape* as "to love, to be full of good-will and exhibit the same."[8] It is the highest form of love. There is no end to God's love. Again, it is not based on performance or merit; therefore, you cannot err so badly that He would stop loving you. God's love is eternal.

God has many names that denote His character and attributes, but I want to look at the very first reference of His name as Elohim in Genesis 1:1. The Hebrew translation for *Elohim* is "Creator."[9] God's overflowing love for mankind was shown by creating all things man needed to enjoy life. As verified in Genesis, chapter one, God prepared everything—the sun, moon, water, fish, vegetation—richly all things to enjoy. All of this was done during the first five days of creation, so it was prepared and waiting for man on the sixth day of creation.

God loves His entire creation; not only man, but everything He created. It was all by the determinate counsel and original purpose and intent that everything we would ever need was provided before man arrived. And since the "decree of the reproductive seed" is still valid in the earth as denoted in Genesis 1:11 with "every seed producing after its own kind," God is faithful to this decree by continually providing for us. No one is exempt from God's goodness, which is inexplicably good!

Just imagine being like a child and receive all that the Father has already prepared for you. What about your birthday, Christmas, anniversary, retirement, etc.? When you are the recipient of a gift, the only thing you need to do is reach out and take possession. Why? It's because the gift giver has already done the work. First, the thought to endow you with the gift has been placed on the giver's heart and mind. The giver is obedient to the prompting of giving you a gift. Remember, the gift recipient does not have to earn it. Once the work to obtain finances to buy the gift is completed, the person then goes shopping for the perfect gift for you. They may wrap the gift in beautiful wrapping paper. Last, the delivery of the package. Wow! So much has gone into what the recipient didn't have to work for. The same with God; this is how much He thought about us by sending His only begotten Son. He is the greatest everlasting gift of all, Jesus Christ. He was wrapped in the most unassuming wrapping, swaddling clothes. (Luke 2)

Since God's love is exemplified in giving, He has given us everything that pertains to life and godliness.

> By his divine power, God has given us everything we need for living a godly life. We have received all of this by coming to know him, the one who called us to himself by means of his marvelous glory and excellence. And because of his glory and excellence, he has given us great and precious promises. These are the promises that enable you to share his divine nature and escape the world's corruption caused by human desires.
>
> 2 Peter 1:3–4 NLT

Speaking of good and precious promises, the promise of sending the Holy Ghost was fulfilled in the book of Acts. When you have an opportunity, please read the entire book of Acts, it is adventurous! Many demonstrations of the Holy Ghost working through God's people were accounted in that book. As you discover more about these documented works, one thing that is most exciting to me is that the Holy Spirit is still helping us today. Jesus first made mention of the promise of the Holy Ghost as shown below.

> Howbeit when he, the Spirit of truth, is come, he will guide you into all truth: for he

shall not speak of himself; but whatsoever he shall hear, *that* shall he speak: and he will shew you things to come. He shall glorify me: for he shall receive of mine, and shall shew *it* unto you.

John 16:13–14

God has given us everything we need on this earth including divine intervention. The Holy Spirit is referred to as "He" which is a part of God's triune being, the Father, Son, and Holy Spirit. Jesus was anointed by the Holy Spirit to be effective while on the earth. As Jesus said in the book of John, chapters 14, 15 and 16, the Holy Spirit is our "Comforter, Teacher, Advocate and Helper; and that He will remain with us forever." The next chapter elaborates on our triune Creator.

Chapter Four

Hebrew Meaning of Number 16

L ove is at the center of everything as it relates to God simply because God is love. As I continued to study more about the love of God and getting more revelation about it for this book, I found that the number 16 in Hebrew is love. Having completed this book in 2016, I felt that was significant and no coincidence so we're going to delve into it a little deeper. The number 16 is a grouping of two Hebrew letters (tev–zayin)[10]. The disciple John wrote in John 3:16, a very familiar scripture, which reveals the mystery of how our Creator expresses His love for us through giving. Because of His great love toward us He gave His only begotten Son. As I mentioned in chapter three regarding the Holy Spirit, our God is triune, God the Father, God the Son, and God the Holy Spirit. These three are in unity and do not contradict. This passage of scripture in John depicts "3" + "16" = Love.

I am amazed at how God is precise in His timing and numbering of everything. There are many occasions in the Bible where numbering is very important. Matt Slick conducted research of several numbers and their meanings in the Bible as shown below.

One of the interesting features of Hebrew

and Greek is that in both written languages there are no numeric characters. Where we have numbers and letters, they have only letters. So, in each language the letters are also used as numbers. In a small way we do the same thing in English. For example, is "O" a zero or a letter in the alphabet? Is "l" a one or a small L? When they are used, the context tells us which is which; and we have no problem understanding it. The same goes for Hebrew and Greek. They knew when they were writing numbers and when they were writing letters. The interesting thing is that when a word is written, it also has a numeric equivalent. For example, the word "Jesus" in Greek is iasous. Since each letter has a numeric equivalent, we can add up each number and get a value. The value is the gammatria. Therefore, the gammatria of "Jesus" in Greek is 888 because i = 10, a = 8, s = 200, o = 70, u = 400, s = 200. There are many interesting 'games' that can be played with this feature of Greek and Hebrew, and much of it is absurd. However, some of the numeric relationships are interesting. Whether or not the numbers really have a significance is still debated in many circles. Nevertheless, I present the information for your examination.[11]

Three	THE NUMBER OF DIVINE PERFECTION. The Trinity consists of Father, Son, and Holy Spirit. There are three qualities of the universe: Time, Space, and Matter. To exist (except for God) all three are required. Each quality consists of three elements. Therefore, we live in a trinity of trinities.

The three qualities of universe are each three:		
Time is one yet three	Space is one yet three	Matter is one yet three
Past Present Future	Height Width Depth	Solid Liquid Gas

We live in a Trinity of Trinities: Romans 1:20 NASB says, "For since the creation of the world His invisible attributes, His eternal power and divine nature have been clearly seen, being understood through what has been made …"

If you are a trichotomist then man is made of three parts:		
Body	Soul	Spirit
Human abilities are three:		
Thought	Word	Deed
The divine attributes are three-fold. God is:		
Omniscient Omnipresent Omnipotent	Love Light Spirit	Holy Righteous Just
Three bear witness (1 John 5:8):		
Spirit	Water	Blood

Christ is Three Shepherds:		
The Good Shepherd (John 10:14-15)--speaking of His death The Great Shepherd (Heb. 13:20)--speaking of His resurrection The Chief Shepherd (1 Pet. 5:4)--speaking of His glory		
The Three appearances of Christ:		
Past: Has appeared (Heb. 9:26) to put away sin Present: Is appearing (Heb. 9:24) in the presence of God Future: Will appear (Heb. 9:28) to those who await Him		
The Father spoke from Heaven three times:		
Matt. 3:17, "This is My beloved Son, in whom I am well pleased." Matt. 17:5, "This is My beloved Son, with whom I am well-pleased; listen to Him." John 12:28, "I have both glorified it [the Father's name], and will glorify it again."		
Both the Tabernacle and the Temple consisted of three parts:		
The Court	The Holy Place	The Sanctuary
Regarding the Tabernacle:		
The Holy of Holies was a cube (10 cubits x 10 cubits x 10 cubits)		
Regarding the Temple:		
The Holy of Holies was a cube (20 cubits x 20 cubits x 20 cubits)[12]		

I am also adding another scriptural reference to accompany 1 John 5:8. It is 1 John 5:7 which tells us about agreement in heaven.

> For there are three that bear record in heaven, the Father, the Word, and the Holy Ghost: and these three are one.

As I mentioned in chapter one, in order to

function as human beings, we are comprised as three-in-one as well. When David penned, "Bless the LORD, O my soul; and all that is within me, bless his holy name" in Psalm 103:1, David was speaking to his soul. Sometimes we may not feel like praising the Lord. But we speak to ourselves regarding other situations. We'll say, "Why did you do that Celeste!" As an outward physical act of our worship to God, we lift our hands, speak with our mouth and raise our voice to praise the Lord, or with our body move around joyfully in various acts of worship. However, each unit that makes up the totality of us is in unison. This is of vital importance. When you are having a conversation with someone, you want their undivided attention. Right? God desires all of us. He gave us all of Him, Father, Son and Holy Spirit, so it is proper that we give Him our all.

Chapter Five

You are Accepted, ReCeive

According as he hath chosen us in him before the foundation of the world, that we should be holy and without blame before him in love: Having predestinated us unto the adoption of children by Jesus Christ to himself, according to the good pleasure of his will, To the praise of the glory of his grace, wherein he hath made us accepted in the beloved. Ephesians 1:4-6

It is not a coincidence that this is chapter five. In biblical numerology, the number five stands for God's grace and favor towards humans. He has accepted you and has given you grace and favor; now receive. Do you remember having a "grace period" for late payments or if you were running late for work or school? It felt so good to have that extended to us.

Well, the grace that God extends to us is through Jesus Christ. He died and rose from the grave so that we can be reconciled to God. This means we have been restored to an amiable relationship with Him. God's love through Jesus Christ is the reconciler. Love gives and protects. For God was in Christ, reconciling the world to himself, no longer counting people's sins against them. And he gave us this wonderful gift of reconciliation that you can read about in 2 Corinthians 5:19 NLT.

When you have been born again (John 3:1–

7) you are accepted by God because of the redemptive blood of Jesus Christ. Therefore, it is not according to our own righteousness or penance; our redemption comes only through Jesus Christ. It is His finished work and all one needs to do is receive His accomplishment.

Some may ask, "How do I gain acceptance?" Here is an example of what I mean by that. Have you ever auditioned for sports, band, choir, applied for college, or a cheerleading squad? Each of these requires you to practice and then "try out" to become a part of the organization. However, in the family of God, you will not have to audition to become a part of the family of God. Ephesians 1:5 says we are adopted as children of God. Children that are adopted through an adoption agency do not have to audition to become a member of a family that chooses them. However, there are certain criteria the prospective parent(s) must meet in order to qualify for adoption.

Thanks be to Father God; He supremely qualifies as an adoptive parent. He passes all background checks; He is able to support us financially, He has the ultimate healthcare plan, and meets every need we will ever have. He also promises "never to leave us nor forsake us" (Hebrews 13:5). We never should feel that we are different from anyone else because we are all adopted by Him and accepted. He loves us equally, and we are all His favorites (Acts 10:34).

> And will be a Father unto you, and ye shall be my sons and daughter saith the Lord Almighty.
>
> 2 Corinthians 6:18

Some people say, "I found the God" but He was never lost. Even when we were sinners, God through Jesus Christ was constantly watching over us and drawing us to Himself. It is impossible for us to come to Christ unless God draws us by His love. Jeremiah writes,

> The LORD hath appeared of old unto me saying, Yea, I have loved thee with an everlasting love: therefore with lovingkindness have I drawn thee.
>
> Jeremiah 31:3

LIVING WATER

There is a story in John 4 about a Samaritan woman at the well. The woman and Jesus did something unexpected and revolutionary—they took a risk. This Samaritan woman was nameless possibly to protect and cover her as only our God ever so gently does. The interesting thing about this story is that the situation that Jesus and this woman found themselves in was a reversal of the usual. My revelation is that this encounter was "flipping the script." Their meeting was a divine appointment and they both took risks to fulfill God's plan for the woman.

A risk occurs when a person sets out to do something and then goes! Jesus was always challenging people to set out to do something out of the ordinary. He told Peter to "come" and walk on the water. To say the least, that certainly was risky!

At their humble beginnings, a risk taker's goal is not necessarily that of being famous or a history maker. For example, Harriet Tubman, a former American slave and leading abolitionist, George Washington Carver, a botanist and inventor, and Thomas Edison along with Lewis Latimer who respectively invented and wrote books about the light bulb passions were not for themselves to gain celebrity status; their passion was to fulfill their assignment and assist others.

Jesus is the perfect example of someone fulfilling His assignment. In John 4, there was an urgency for Him to get to the woman. I believe her heart was crying out to God. She had a divine appointment and did not know her life was about to change for the better. According to John 8:28, Jesus does nothing unless His Father instructs Him. The Samaritans were not looked upon favorably by the Jews. They were considered a mixed race of half-Jews and were outcasts. Unfortunately, much like the racism prevalent even today. To avoid Samaria, the Jews would travel around it via the Jordan River. However, Jesus shared with His disciples that He needed to go through Samaria.

The direct route to Samaria from Judea and Galilee was seventy miles or a two and half days walk. Since many of the Jews chose not to go through Samaria, they traveled the hot desert road from Jerusalem to Jericho and up the Jordan valley. They did this because of their disdain for the Samaritans. They journeyed almost twice the distance on a much hotter and more uncomfortable road. But Jesus cut right through the narrow-minded prejudice and went through Samaria.

Let's picture the scene for a moment. It is 12:00 noon. Jesus is thirsty and tired. I am sure Jesus and His disciples were exhausted. Today, when we travel in a vehicle for fifty miles, we make a rest stop. I will not dare mention running a 26.2-mile marathon. Some of you might even faint at the thought. Wherever Jesus went, it was for a purpose. Jesus knew she would be coming to the well at that exact moment. Nothing is coincidental. The woman was not looking for Jesus, but Jesus was expecting her. Although she did not realize it, the woman had a "divine appointment" with the Son of God. (In another chapter, I talk about not missing your appointment.) When Jesus arrived at the well, He saw the woman and asked her for a drink of water. She was astonished that He being a Jew was actually speaking to her. But Jesus shared with her that if she knew the wonderful gift of God that He had for her and who it was that was asking her for a drink that she would ask Him for "Living Water." She pondered logically and supposed that was a great proposition to not come to the well so often. Then Jesus explained the spiritual meaning of Living Water and that He would give to the extent that she would never be thirsty again. It would be a perpetual spring of water in her spirit that would eternally refresh her. Finally, she asked for the Living Water so she would not have to make the long trip to draw water.

There was a plan to turn this woman's life around. Jesus had a word of knowledge and told her about her past and current situation. He told her that she had been married five times and was now living with a man. She had a sketchy past, and her current circumstances did not look any better. The woman perceived that Jesus was a prophet. The woman received a prophetic word in one of the most unlikely places, not on the mountains where her forefathers worshiped, not in church service, not at a prayer breakfast, not at the singles ministry gathering. She received her Word at the well. Although that is an unusual place to get a prophetic word, once my son and I were at the grocery store and we both received a prophetic word. It is possible that the woman had been praying a prayer like this, "Oh Lord, I need a sign and need to hear from you. I have been married five times. I am tired of this lifestyle. I want to be free from living with this man who is not my husband. I am tired of being ostracized, criticized, marginalized, disrespected and rejected. I am looking for love in all the wrong places. My man is too lazy and won't get the water. The man I'm shacking up with boasts that I should be glad to have a man. Oh Lord, I am poor and I need him so I can pay my bills. I need to hear from you!" Historically, she knew per her ancestors that it was prophesied that the Messiah (Jesus) would come. Then Jesus boldly proclaimed, "I Am the Messiah!" (John 4:26 TLB).

The woman was so excited and ran from the well and into the village stating, "come and meet a man who told me everything I ever did! Can this be the Messiah?" (John 4:28-29 TLB).

I believe Jesus' risk-taking mission was accomplished with many positive outcomes. To highlight a few, He took a risk and challenged the status quo by going through Samaria and reaching those perceived as outcasts. This was achieved by liberating the woman who was dealing with rejection and stigmatization. Because of her past, I am sure everyone in town knew who she was. The women were probably jealous or fearful that she might steal their man. Then after her encounter with Jesus, she immediately became His promoter, and her responsibility was to share the good news! He trusted her with telling others about Him.

Just as there was a plan for the woman of Samaria, there is a plan for you. What is your circumstance that only God knows about? A meeting with the Master with the opportunity to change your life and the lives of others forever is available for the asking. Have you ever been identified or labeled by what you have been through? God is not trying to (as they say) "put you on front street." He desires to put you on display for His glory to take you to the top. God draws us, not drives us to Himself. It does not matter the current or past condition of your life because everyone has missed the mark at some point in their lives. (Romans 3:23) His love will meet you where you are. You are worthy. "Perfect" people need not apply.

LONGSUFFERING

There are many instances where God has dealt very patiently with mankind meaning He is longsuffering. We learned in the Old Testament in several instances that God's longsuffering eventually ended. There is a difference between love and longsuffering. Longsuffering is showing patience in spite of the disloyalty of someone. The fulfillment of God's promise to Noah in Genesis, chapters 6 and 7, and to the cities Sodom and Gomorrah in Genesis 18 and 19 denote how His longsuffering reached an end. Eventually, God's longsuffering will culminate for those who have rejected His Son, Jesus Christ. But in contrast, His love for you will never end. Although His love is everlasting, let us not despise His forbearance and longsuffering. It is the Lord's goodness that leads to repentance (Romans 2:4). Receive His love and His longsuffering.

ReCeive!

Actually, I received an awesome revelation from God in regards to the word "receive." He said, "Divide the word *receive* into two syllables, *re* and *ceive*." The definition of *re* is "that the performance of the new action brings back an earlier state of affairs."[13] The definition of *ceive* comes from Latin, where it has the meaning of "get, receive."[14] This meaning is found in such words as CONCEIVE, DECEIVE, TRANSCEIVER.

Here is the revelation…God's purposeful mission through Jesus Christ was accomplished before the foundation of the world (Revelation 13:8). Since God begins with the end in mind, He has completed the work through the performance of bringing back an earlier state of affairs. This was God's original intent for mankind to live a life of freedom, health and prosperity.

> Declaring the end from the beginning, and from ancient times *the things* that are not *yet* done, saying, My counsel shall stand, and I will do all my pleasure:

> Isaiah 46:10

It is only through the shed blood of Jesus Christ, which God planned from the beginning (Hebrews 9:22).

We must be in covenant with Jesus Christ by believing, accepting, and receiving His finished work. Some may ask, "How do I receive?" First, hear God's Word. Then, believe God's Word. Faith will continually come by hearing His Word to receive His promises (Romans 10:17). The call to action is to receive!

The next time you see, hear or declare the word "receive," think about what it really means to receive. Any news that someone shares with you could be good or evil. Your goal is to make the appropriate decision depending on what is shared. If you receive it, fully receive it. If you do not receive it, fully repel it! The doctor may diagnose and deliver an unfavorable report. Declare, "I do not receive that diagnosis. I receive the report of the Lord." (Isaiah 53:1–5) Receive your healing that was paid for by Jesus Christ with His precious blood. This also includes receiving your deliverance for your soul from depression, oppression, perversion, toxic thinking, gender confusion, etc.

Let us look at receiving from another perspective particularly when God gives you a direct opportunity to make a choice for you and your family. It is written:

> "Today I have given you the choice between life and death, between blessings and curses. Now I call on heaven and earth to witness the choice you make. Oh, that you would choose life, so that you and your descendants might live!"

> Deuteronomy 30:19 NLT

The choice is yours. When you yield to God's Holy Spirit, there is absolutely nothing that you have done that the blood of Jesus Christ cannot cleanse. His love reaches you at your lowest point and at the apex of your life. It is nothing you have done to motivate God to love you. Romans 3:23 tells us "For all have sinned." However, through the blood of Jesus Christ, we all have redemption.

> For all have sinned, and come short of the glory of God; Being justified freely by his grace through the redemption that is in Christ Jesus: Whom God hath set forth to be a propitiation through faith in his blood, to declare his righteousness for the remission of sins that are past, through the forbearance of God;

Roman 3:23–25

On the hill called Golgotha where Jesus Christ was being crucified, the naysayers, crucifixion employees, and those who took part in the unjustly imposed guilty verdict gathered while Jesus Christ said, "Father forgive them for they know not what they do" (Luke 23:34). They were ignorant of what they were doing. However, Jesus prayed a priest's prayer for them. Such love!

Chapter Six

How's Your Soil?

"Listen! A farmer went out to plant some seed. As he scattered it across his field, some of the seed fell on a footpath, and the birds came and ate it. Other seed fell on shallow soil with underlying rock. The seed sprouted quickly because the soil was shallow. But the plant soon wilted under the hot sun, and since it didn't have deep roots, it died. Other seed fell among thorns that grew up and choked out the tender plants so they produced no grain. Still other seeds fell on fertile soil, and they sprouted, grew, and produced a crop that was thirty, sixty, and even a hundred times as much as had been planted!" Then he said, "Anyone with ears to hear should listen and understand." Mark 4:3-9 NLT

In this story or parable in Mark 4, Jesus Christ teaches about a sower, seed, and four types of soil. This parable is so simplistic that Jesus said in verse 13, "Know ye not this parable? And how then will you know all parables?" Even a child can understand it.

When I was a little girl, we had a class project in school where we planted seeds in soil in a small cup. We placed the cup on the windowsill so that it could get sunlight. We were so excited and had great anticipation as we watered the cups for several weeks. Then finally, we witnessed a small green leaf break through the soil. As students, there were important factors we had to consider. It was essential that we had good soil (extremely key), water, fertilizer, and the environmental condition had to be conducive to grow the plant.

In agriculture, seeds are planted into good soil, water is added, and sometimes the soil may need fertilizer for additional nutrients. The germination process begins in the soil's dark and moist environment. Sometimes foreign invaders such as weeds and pests must be extricated. Finally, after the proper care the plant, tree or produce that was planted will grow to benefit yourself and others.

This parable speaks of various types of soil. When we allow the seed, which is God's Word to be planted and germinated in our spirit and soul, the Word can grow and become firmly rooted in our hearts so that we can receive nourishment in and through the times of testing.

Our spirit and soul are symbolic of soil. We receive God's life-giving Word in our heart, which is the deep and innermost part where only God sees and fully understands. He "knows our thoughts afar off," (as referenced a little later in this book) and has experienced all that we may encounter.

> Now that we know what we have—Jesus, this great High Priest with ready access to God—let's not let it slip through our fingers. We don't have a priest who is out of touch with our reality. He's been through weakness and testing, experienced it all— all but the sin. So, let's walk right up to him and get what he is so ready to give. Take the mercy, accept the help.
>
> Hebrews 4:15–16 *The Message*

A tree or plant that is firmly planted will not waver when strong winds and rains come. Therefore, when we allow our roots to go deeply into good ground, we will not waver because the soil of our heart is conducive to the seed being firmly established and nurtured. The Lord always watches over His Word (seed) to perform all of it. God's Word never returns to Him negated but accomplishes everything He delights and prospers where His Word is sent (Isaiah 55:11). The Lord ensures us that in the end, everything will work out fine. Life may throw you curve balls, and things may not seem good right now, but all things are working for your good. The progressive work of the process is guaranteed in God's Word that the final outcome is good (Romans 8:28). God loves you too much to leave you without help. He has begun a good work in you and He will perform or complete it (Philippians 1:6). Therefore, the work in you or "harvest" is like a farmer who works in his field until he gathers the harvest that will sustain him for months. God makes it so simple for us to understand. We do not need to complicate His impeccable plan. Remember, it all began in a garden; the garden of Eden.

Therefore, when we come to God in the volume of the book that is written of us (as Paul said in Hebrews 10:7) are we fulfilling our personalized book that God has authored expressly for us to do His will? As various species of foliage needs a certain amount of exposure to sun, shade, minimal water, lots of water, and fertilizer to grow to its fullest potential to benefit us, we also have our book to fulfill. One of my assignments was to complete the writing of this book. I am loving this journey. My hope is to die empty that means that I have completed every mandate my Creator has given me in this life.

Throughout the world, there have been many great inventions. The creators of those technologies wrote manuals in regards to their operation and potentiality. So why not go to the One who created us and inquire about our ability and purpose? Everything has the potentiality of preeminence in industries. Who is stopping you? Could it, be you? What is preventing you from moving forward? Is it a job that you are overqualified for? Would you like to travel but you are afraid of flying? Are you looking at the outward appearance of a potential wife or husband? Try not to judge too quickly. In a movie that came out a few years ago called *Coming to America* that is exactly what happened. The main character was a prince, but no one around him knew it. Maybe it is a ministry that you need to launch. There are souls waiting to hear your voice.

FULL OF MERCY

God is rich in mercy. Some may say, "How can God be merciful seeing there are many dreadful things happening in the world, and God does nothing about it?" He has given us dominion and made us stewards over the earth as was outlined in Genesis 1. Jesus Christ has redeemed us, and He took back everything that Adam handed over to Satan through high treason. When you are a steward over an owner's property or possessions, it is incumbent upon you to know what the owner's preference is as well as what they approve or disapprove of. Therefore, we must stay connected to God to hear His heart and feel the pulse of what He desires. He is always for the best and not the worst. In Jeremiah, the Lord declares that He demonstrates unfailing love and brings justice to the earth.

> This is what the Lord says: "Don't let the wise boast in their wisdom, or the powerful boast in their power, or the rich boast in their riches. But those who wish to boast should boast in this alone: that they truly know me and understand that I am the Lord who demonstrates unfailing love and who brings justice and righteousness to the earth, and that I delight in these things. I, the Lord, have spoken!"

> Jeremiah 9:23–24 NLT

When the gospel or good news of Jesus Christ is presented to you, receive it in your spirit. Take God at His Word because He cannot be separated from His Word (John 1:1). He is His Word. Disclosure and understanding come from hearing and receiving the good news by faith. The question you have to ask yourself is, do you trust Him? Are you aware of God's purpose and original intent for you? It is not that He does not care about you or His world. It is imperative that we exercise our dominion. We must not be distracted by what the powers of darkness are doing in wreaking havoc. Jesus told us we are salt and light sent into a dark world; therefore, that is what we must attain.

> "You are the salt of the earth. But what good is salt if it has lost its flavor? Can you make it salty again? It will be thrown out and trampled underfoot as worthless. You are the light of the world—like a city on a hilltop that cannot be hidden. No one lights a lamp and then puts it under a basket. Instead, a lamp is placed on a stand, where it gives light to everyone in the house. In the same way, let your

good deeds shine out for all to see, so that everyone will praise your heavenly Father."

Matthew 5:13–16 NLT

In the Old Testament, there are types and shadows or figures of things to come. In the book of Leviticus, chapter 16, the life of Jesus Christ and His sinless blood was represented. In this account, there was a ceremony to remit sins and errors of the priest and of the people that was completed every year by sprinkling the blood of sacrificed animals on the mercy seat. So, we find that Jesus Christ, who is our High Priest, has sprinkled His own blood in heaven. The writer in Hebrews states,

> For Christ is not entered into the holy places made with hands, *which* are the figures of the true; but into heaven itself, now to appear in the presence of God for us: nor yet that he should offer himself often, as the high priest entereth into the holy place every year with blood of others; for then must he often have suffered since the foundation of the world: but now once in the end of the world hath he appeared to put away sin by the sacrifice of himself. And as it is appointed unto men once to die, but after this the judgment: so, Christ was once offered to bear the sins of many; and unto them that look for him shall he appear the second time without sin unto salvation.

Hebrews 9:24–28

The mercy seat is a reminder of the finished work of Christ and the sacrifice of His own blood once and for all on Calvary's cross. The Lord is not willing that anyone would perish (separated eternally); He is longsuffering. We all have an opportunity to repent and accept the finished work of Christ. Here is evidence.

> The Lord is not slack concerning his promise, as some men count slackness; but is longsuffering to us-ward, not willing that any should perish, but that all should come to repentance.

> 2 Peter 3:9

To delve deeper into God's masterful plan, you may ask, why did God send His only son, why Jesus' blood, and why us? I submit to you that we are worth it all. It is not that we deserve it. Surely, that is not reason. We were all born guilty (Psalm 51:5) in sin. Even if you were born and placed in a controlled environment with no opportunity to commit any act of sin, nor ever heard the gospel of Jesus Christ, you are still in sin because of how you were born. But here is the elaborate yet simple plan of hope:

> Therefore, since we have been made right in God's sight by faith, we have peace with God because of what Jesus Christ our Lord has done for us. Because of our faith, Christ has brought us into this place of undeserved privilege where we now stand, and we confidently and joyfully look forward to sharing God's glory. We can rejoice, too, when we run into problems and trials, for we know that they help us develop endurance. And endurance develops strength of character, and character strengthens our confident hope of salvation. And this hope will not lead to

disappointment. For we know how dearly God loves us, because he has given us the Holy Spirit to fill our hearts with his love. When we were utterly helpless, Christ came at just the right time and died for us sinners. Now, most people would not be willing to die for an upright person, though someone might perhaps be willing to die for a person who is especially good. But God showed his great love for us by sending Christ to die for us while we were still sinners. And since we have been made right in God's sight by the blood of Christ, he will certainly save us from God's condemnation. For since our friendship with God was restored by the death of his Son while we were still his enemies, we will certainly be saved through the life of his Son. So now we can rejoice in our wonderful new relationship with God because our Lord Jesus Christ has made us friends of God.

Adam and Christ Contrasted

When Adam sinned, sin entered the world. Adam's sin brought death, so death spread to everyone, for everyone sinned. Yes, people sinned even before the law was given. But it was not counted as sin because there was not yet any law to break. Still, everyone died—from the time of Adam to the time of Moses—even those who did not disobey an explicit commandment of God, as Adam did. Now Adam is a symbol, a representation of Christ, who was yet to come. But there is a great difference between Adam's sin and God's gracious gift. For the sin of this one man, Adam, brought death to many. But even greater is God's wonderful grace and his gift of forgiveness to many through this other man, Jesus Christ. And the result of God's gracious gift is very different from the result of that one man's sin. For Adam's sin led to condemnation, but God's free gift leads to our being made right with God, even though we are guilty of many sins. For the sin of this one man, Adam, caused death to rule over many. But even greater is God's wonderful grace and his gift of righteousness, for all who receive it will live in triumph over sin and death through this one man, Jesus Christ. Yes, Adam's one sin brings condemnation for everyone, but Christ's one act of righteousness brings a right relationship with God and new life for everyone. Because one person disobeyed God, many became sinners. But because one other person obeyed God, many will be made righteous. God's law was given so that all people could see how sinful they were. But as people sinned more and more, God's wonderful grace became more abundant. So just as sin ruled over all people and brought them to death, now God's wonderful grace rules instead, giving us right standing with God and resulting in eternal life through Jesus Christ our Lord.

Romans 5 NLT

Although people will say that their various religions and beliefs gain them access to God the Father, or "Well, we all serve the same God. However, Jesus Christ the infallible Word tells us,

"Jesus told him, 'I am the way, the truth, and the life. No one can come to the Father except through me'" (John 14:6 NLT).

Chapter Seven

Father God's Love

See what an incredible quality of love the Father has shown to us, that we would [be permitted to] be named and called and counted the children of God! 1 John 3:1 AMP

God's love is the ultimate, supreme love. Like me, some people may not know their biological father, but I can truly say unashamedly, that my heavenly Father is my Father. I am being fathered from above. Some characteristics that epitomize a loving father are unconditional, protective, providential, supportive, disciplinary, instructive, exemplary, and developmental. His love assures us that all is well.

Check this out. God's love is first to the entire universe. He loves everything He created. He provides sunshine, rain, crops, and everything in nature for all to enjoy. However, the greatest thing He has given to everyone is an opportunity to receive His Son, Jesus Christ (John 3:16). Think about it. Jesus can be our big brother!

> God, for whom and through whom everything was made, chose to bring many children into glory. And it was only right that he should make Jesus, through his suffering, a perfect leader, fit to bring them into their salvation. So now Jesus and the ones he makes holy have the same

Father. That is why Jesus is not ashamed to call them his brothers and sisters. For he said to God, "I will proclaim your name to my brothers and sisters. I will praise you among your assembled people."

Hebrews 2:10–12 NLT

This is exciting news. However, when you receive Jesus Christ, then God becomes your Father through adoption.

For ye have not received the spirit of bondage again to fear; but ye have received the Spirit of adoption, whereby we cry, Abba, Father. The Spirit itself beareth witness with our spirit, that we are the children of God: And if children, then heirs; heirs of God, and joint-heirs with Christ; if so be that we suffer with *him*, that we may be also glorified together.

Romans 8:15–17

According to *Strong's Concordance*, the Greek word for *father* (pro gene ator) is "patér."[15] *HELPS™ Word-studies* definitions for father are:

patér – father; one who imparts life and is committed to it; a progenitor, bringing into being to pass on the potential for likeness.[16]

patér ("father") is used of our heavenly Father. He imparts life, from physical birth to the gift of eternal life through the second birth (regeneration, being born again). Through ongoing sanctification, the believer more and more resembles their heavenly Father – i.e. each time they receive faith from Him and obey it, which results in their unique glorification.[17]

Salvation is a free gift we do nothing to earn it. According to Ephesians, we are saved by the grace of God, His unmerited favor.

> God saved you by his grace when you believed. And you can't take credit for this; it is a gift from God. Salvation is not a reward for the good things we have done, so none of us can boast about it.

> Ephesians 2:8–9 NLT

Our inheritance as children is His love. We become a part of His family. Consider a newborn baby. The baby does not earn their parents love by good behavior as they progress through life. The parent's love is free; it is unconditional. The baby is loved and protected, and the child's parents prepared for its comfort well in advance of the baby's birth. This is how God sees us before we are born into His family. We will never be an orphan.

An orphan is someone whose parents have died. The person can experience a great sense of abandonment, loneliness, and rejection. All of these emotions are extensions of many other byproducts of dysfunction such as a victim mentality and the inability to have wholesome, loving relationships. Often anger, fear and poverty manifest in their lives. All of these result in an orphan spirit. Remember everything begins in the spirit realm and the mind.

The good news is that we have been adopted by God. David wrote in Psalm 27:10, "when my father and my mother forsake me, then the LORD will take me up." In *Strong's Concordance*, the word *forsake* in the Hebrew language is "azab."[18] It translates, "to depart from, leave behind, leave, let alone."[19] Will you allow God to become your

Father? He is not a man that is waiting for you to make a mistake and punish you like a dictatorial maniac. God can become your loving Father. Although people may reject you, please know and understand they did not create you. They really do not know the "real you." You, as well as they, were created to be godlike.

Sometimes we may "miss the mark" or commit a sinful act after becoming a member of the family of God. This is not the time to run from God but run to Him. He is a "very present help in time of trouble" (Psalm 46:1). When I became a young adult, I strayed from the Lord and became promiscuous. I was looking for love and acceptance in all the wrong places—relationships and individuals. When you miss it, do not get stuck there; keep walking by faith. Keep trusting in God as your heavenly Father. He has begun a good work in you, and will complete it until the end (Philippians 1:6). When we do not trust God as I AM THAT I AM (Exodus 3:14), this is a form of unbelief. Even unbelief is sin. Do not despair, repent to God, ask for forgiveness (remember the shed blood of Jesus cleanses us) and He will forgive you. Remember, "a just *man* falleth seven times, and riseth up again" (Proverbs 24:16). It is God's desire that you do not sin and not deter your journey with condemnation. Here is proof.

> My little children, these things write I unto you, that ye sin not. And if any man sin, we have an advocate with the Father, Jesus Christ the righteous: And he is the propitiation for our sins: and not for ours only, but also for the sins of the whole world.
>
> 1 John 2:1–2

The weight of condemnation and fear will keep you from taking action to move forward with your life. Condemnation reminds us of former disappointments, our flaws (everyone has them), or anxieties about the future. Do not let your past dictate your future. Someone may be reading this book in prison. Life is not over for you. As long as there is life within you, there is hope. When you lose your hope, you lose your ability to move forward. The Bible says, "Hope deferred makes the heart sick, but when desire is fulfilled, it is a tree of life" (Proverbs 13:12 AMP). Young people, you may be experiencing bullying at school or during extracurricular activities. Others may experience a hostile environment at work with workplace bullies. The peace of God is available to you for the asking. Recognize, accept and receive the love that God lavishly pours on you daily that drives out fear. Jesus said in John 14:27, "Peace I leave with you, my peace I give unto you: not as the world giveth, give I unto you. Let not your heart be troubled, neither let it be afraid."

God loves us so much. Do you know of any fathers who would sacrifice their son for the sake of the entire world? As a reminder, John 1:14 reveals that the "Word was made flesh" and the Word is Jesus Christ. God put His deity aside, came in the flesh and walked the earth as a man empowered by the Holy Spirit. There are many references in the Word of God that confirms how Jesus lived on the earth, anointed by God as a man. To demonstrate how we should live as the Holy Spirit leads, guides, and empowers us as born again believers, here is a powerful reference in God's Word.

How God anointed Jesus of Nazareth with

the Holy Ghost and with power: who went about doing good, and healing all that were oppressed of the devil; for God was with him.

Acts 10:38

Chapter Eight

God's Girls

Most of us have heard this statement, "looking for love in all the wrong places" so I want to challenge you. Are you looking for that knight in shining armor or Boaz? Maybe you thought you found your Boaz but instead, a wolf in sheep's clothing showed up. Has your Dr. Jekyll turned into Mr. Hyde? Ladies, it is time for us to know our worth! You are a masterpiece. Some of you do know your worth. However, some still seek their value through the excellent workmanship of designers such as Louis Vuitton®, COACH®, Dooney & Bourke™, Gucci®, Chanel®, MICHAEL KORS® and the beautiful shoes, fragrances and clothing they produce. But really, who are you? Are these designers worthy of YOU wearing their goods? You may love yourself. But do you like yourself? You are more valuable than what you wear, what you carry and whom you advertise when you wear it. It is imperative that you realize the priceless value of who you are, to God and yourself. Once you do, you can exhibit this self-worth to others who will respect and value you. Ask God to help you realize His Word in Psalm 139 for yourself (I have provided the entire Psalm just for you at the end of the chapter). You have to be good to you and put yourself first. Take yourself to dinner. Be confident. A man validating you does not establish your life. It is important first to appreciate yourself, and then you will know how a man should regard you.

Why are women looking for men anyway? The Bible states, "the man who finds a wife finds a treasure, and he receives favor from the LORD" (Proverbs 18:22 NLT). This means when he finds you, he "discovers" you. Some say, "Girl, I'm going to find me a man at so and so place," but by nature, men like to hunt. They like to tinker, explore and learn. To be a wife before you get married is to be appropriate and complete. Be ready to be presented when your man finds you. God prepared Eve and made her suitable for Adam. Again, the scripture in Proverbs says men will "obtain favor from the LORD." Let me speak a word to the men for a minute. Men, you may be fearful yet desire to be the head of the wife, the family's provider and lead them. Do not fear that you are on your own after you find your wife. He will show you how to be all that the family needs you to be. God promises that you will obtain favor from Him.

The only time a woman should be hunting and searching is on shopping excursions. When a woman looks for a man, her approach is perceived as solicitation. In terms of female prostitution, these are women who look for and beckon men. They have put themselves on display for sale or exploitation. Sometimes, the women are not soliciting for themselves per se but out of necessity in other words to have a "roof over their head," food, or making money for the pimp who is exploiting them. They try to meet their need because the order that God ordained for men and women has been distorted. The result of this disorder is a desperation and fear in their soul. Their reality screams to them that there is no way out.

Other distortions of God's natural order are

women being viewed by some men (who do not respect them) as sex objects to fondle, use, abuse, consume like a juicy steak, and discard instead of regard. There are also some women have turned to another woman for relationship and intimacy either out of disgust for men or possibly the lack thereof. This absolutely is not the answer. This distortion goes against a woman's nature and how we were created. Woman was made for man, not another woman. A perverse spirit is the driving force which goes against a Holy God and the laws of nature. Mankind has strayed away from God's natural order and original intent. Some people are dissatisfied or perplexed about their sexuality, and this opens the door for Satan. He does not bring life, only death and destruction.

Even from the beginning of time in the garden of Eden until now, Satan's goal is to destroy women. Women are the womb of society. We are the legal entry of life. No human being would have been birthed into the earth realm without a woman. If the destructible plan of Satan were accomplished, God's mandate to us, "be fruitful, multiply and replenish the earth" would end.

Women are strong, we are the carriers of life, we are nurturers, we are intuitive, and we are warriors to carry out what is on God's heart. Our wholeness depends on future generations to be whole. Please do not pay any credence to the devil or his angels. They are not legal in the earth realm; because He was not birthed by woman. It is important that we hear and obey the voice of God and follow Him. As God's child, the voice of Satan is a stranger to you, and you should not follow it. I decree and declare; you only hear the voice of the Good Shepherd and a stranger you will not follow.

DON'T MISS YOUR OPPORTUNITY

You are dear and valued as God's tender creation. There are too many little girls, young ladies and mature women saying internally and thinking, "choose me, choose me, I am beautiful, I am a loving person, I am respectable, I am worthy!" Focus on doing the work of the Lord and present your request to Him. He will wonderfully surprise you with the desires of your heart.

There is a cry of desperation, hurt, and disappointment coming from so many that have been hurt by being out of God's perfect order. Let's dissect this word *disappointment*. The prefix *dis* is defined as a Latin prefix meaning "apart," "asunder," "away," "utterly," or "having a privative, negative, or reversing force."[20]Other words with this prefix are disconnect, disassemble, disease, disability, disbelief, discontent, dishearten, dislike, and disown. The prefix *dis* is a separator from the intended purpose of these words. I am sure you have had some disappointments, which means a separated or missed appointment schedule for your life.

I want to encourage you; do not miss your appointment! The thoughts God has toward you are "thoughts of peace, and not of evil, to give you an expected end" (Jeremiah 29:11). Meet your appointment; you will not be disappointed. Life is too short to live it by "trial and error." The devil does not want you to succeed. But, God always causes you to triumph (2 Corinthians 2:14). The Lord will have you at the right place and at the right time for the right man. Come into divine alignment with God with your spirit (salvation), soul (mind, will, emotions, intellect), and body (present your body as a living sacrifice to God) and you will prove His good, acceptable and perfect will for your life (Romans 12:1–2).

We all have scars with a story to tell of how they happened; some scars are visible, and some are not. We should never let circumstances dictate who we are. Father God loves us so much and is the healer of brokenness whether it's our hearts, spirits or physical ailments. He heals any brokenness in our lives. It is His will that we are in a totality of health in our spirit, soul and body.

> And the very God of peace sanctify you wholly; and *I pray God* your whole spirit and soul and body be preserved blameless unto the coming of our Lord Jesus Christ.
>
> 1 Thessalonians 5:23

I want to admonish you that if you ever feel ashamed, embarrassed or not willing to confide in anyone, please reconsider. Do not allow your inner thoughts and external influences prevent you from speaking to a trusted confidant who can help you. The devil is a liar and desires to silence you, keep you in bondage and full of fear. Fear is not of God. The Bible tells us that "there is no fear in love; but perfect love casteth out fear: because fear hath torment. He that feareth is not made perfect in love. We love him, because he first loved us" (1 John 4:18–19).

Fear paralyzes and causes people to make insensible decisions. Sometimes when an unfortunate event happens, we attribute it to life choices or circumstances beyond our control in which there is complete innocence. Consequently, many feel like an isolated victim feeling violated and abandoned. In some social environments, there are acceptable behaviors called "survival." Survival is a person's reality to do whatever is necessary. Despite whatever has occurred in your life, there is hope! God wants you to do more than survive; He wants you to thrive. Do not give up.

Let God heal the deepest part of your soul. This is where pain likes to hide and come out at the most inconvenient times. Allow the light of God to expose pain, disappointment, fear and insecurities. Sometimes we all lose our way. The great news is that you will find your way through life's journey to fulfill your purpose to reach your God-given destiny.

Can you imagine this? You are a single microscopic sperm out of more than 250 million spermatozoa that swam to fertilize your mother's ovum Even then you were stronger than you could ever imagine. Against all odds, an invisible God assisted you on your journey. From the formation in your mother's womb, until now, the Lord has never left you. Neither will He forsake you; you and God got this! Especially when you have the ultimate Helper, the Holy Ghost. The Holy Ghost is referred to as the "Spirit of truth." He is the Promise that Jesus Christ sent us for help and guidance.

> Howbeit when he, the Spirit of truth, is come, he will guide you into all truth: for he shall not speak of himself; but whatsoever he shall hear, that shall he speak: and he will shew you things to come.

> John 16:13

Square your shoulders and believe God to guide you to victory. It takes only one step. That step is to Jesus Christ. Just think, before you knew yourself, God knew you. He entrusts you with yourself. You are never from God's presence. Even now you are on God's mind. As I promised, here is the entire Psalm 139. I pray that as you meditate it, you let it bring peace and reassurance to you.

Psalm 139 NIV

You have searched me, LORD, and you know me. You know when I sit and when I rise; you perceive my thoughts from afar. You discern my going out and my lying down; you are familiar with all my ways. Before a word is on my tongue you, LORD, know it completely. You hem me in behind and before, and you lay your hand upon me. Such knowledge is too wonderful for me, too lofty for me to attain. Where can I go from your Spirit? Where can I flee from your presence? If I go up to the heavens, you are there; if I make my bed in the depths, you are there. If I rise on the wings of the dawn, if I settle on the far side of the sea, even there your hand will guide me, your right hand will hold me fast If I say, "Surely the darkness will hide me and the light become night around me," even the darkness will not be dark to you; the night will shine like the day, for darkness is as light to you. For you created my inmost being; you knit me together in my mother's womb. I praise you because I am fearfully and wonderfully made; your works are wonderful, I know that full well. My frame was not hidden from you when I was made in the secret place, when I was woven together in the depths of the earth. Your eyes saw my unformed body; all the days ordained for me were written in your book before one of them came to be. How precious to me are your thoughts, God! How vast is the sum of them! Were I to count them, they would outnumber the grains of sand—when I awake, I am still with you. If only you, God, would slay the wicked! Away from me, you who are bloodthirsty! They speak of you with evil intent; your adversaries misuse your name. Do I not hate those who hate you, Lord, and abhor those who are in rebellion against you? I have nothing but hatred for them; I count them my enemies. Search me, God, and know my heart; test me and know my anxious thoughts. See if there is any offensive way in me, and lead me in the way everlasting.

Chapter Nine

Our Social Responsibility

Then shall the King say unto them on his right hand, Come, ye blessed of my Father, inherit the kingdom prepared for you from the foundation of the world: For I was an hungred, and ye gave me meat: I was thirsty, and ye gave me drink: I was a stranger, and ye took me in: Naked, and ye clothed me: I was sick, and ye visited me: I was in prison, and ye came unto me. Then shall the righteous answer him, saying, Lord, when saw we thee an hungred, and fed thee? or thirsty, and gave thee drink? When saw we thee a stranger, and took thee in? or naked, and clothed thee? Or when saw we thee sick, or in prison, and came unto thee? And the King shall answer and say unto them, Verily I say unto you, Inasmuch as ye have done it unto one of the least of these my brethren, ye have done it unto me.

Matthew 25:34–40

God gets involved when we get involved. We are an extension of Him. When you put His will into motion, He starts to work. We are His Body, consisting of hands, feet, etc. He directs us to the right place, at the right time and with the right tools. We do not operate solely in our own ability. God is looking for availability. We are ministers who work with and for God to do His good pleasure.

Each of us has a part to play for His will to be done. We work together like an assembly line. The Bible teaches,

> Who then is Paul, and who *is* Apollos, but ministers by whom ye believed, even as the Lord gave to every man? I have planted, Apollos watered; but God gave the increase. So then neither is he that planteth any thing, neither he that watereth; but God that giveth the increase. Now he that planteth and he that watereth are one: and every man shall receive his own reward according to his own labour. For we are labourers together with God: ye are God's husbandry, *ye are* God's building.
>
> 1 Corinthians 3:5–9

When we do not operate in the divine, supernatural ability, we are relying only on our natural five senses. It is by faith in God's Word, which are His promises that are absolute with no gray areas (2 Corinthians 5:20). Will you allow God to use you as His chosen vessel as an extension of His love?

It is God's will that we are loved, healed, delivered, and released from the bondages of Satan such as addictions, depression, anxiety attacks, diseases, infirmities and illnesses. Everywhere Jesus Christ traveled, He shifted the circumstances and atmosphere for goodwill, healing and deliverance. His purpose was to come as the son of man to destroy the devil's work of wreaking havoc. What are the works of the devil? We can find them here.

> The thief cometh not, but for to steal, and to kill, and to destroy: I am come that they

might have life, and that they might have *it* more abundantly.

John 10:10

The only way we can accomplish our social responsibility is through compassion. Compassion is not sympathy. It is a force that comes from the heart of God and God is love. That force of love compels you to be kind and take action on someone's behalf. The entire chapter of 1 Corinthians 13 is devoted to showing love in excellency. On the earth, Jesus Christ operated as a man doing what His Father instructed Him. He set an example of how we are to function with His Spirit guiding us. The Bible says, "But whoso hath this world's good, and seeth his brother have need, and shutteth up his bowels *of compassion* from him, how dwelleth the love of God in him? My little children, let us not love in word, neither in tongue; but in deed and in truth" (1 John 3:17–18). There are many accounts where Jesus was moved with compassion. That is love in action. Has anyone ever crossed your mind and you prayed for that person or called to check on him or her? This is the prompting of the Holy Ghost for you to take action.

LOVE IN ACTION

In 2014, during the summer I was a part of a prayer evangelism team. Our assignment was to do prayer walks through the North Lawndale neighborhood. It was a neighborhood with one of the highest violent crime rates and impoverished areas in the city of Chicago. We were encouraged to pray for anyone who desired prayer or salvation. One day my team encountered young teenage boys who looked very innocent and unassertive.

We spoke with them and asked if they would like prayer. They wholeheartedly said, "Yes." Can you guess what they requested? They asked that we pray that they make it home alive. They did not ask for the latest Play Station game system, a bike or other materialistic things. This was a real-life concern for them. Everyday life consisted of dodging bullets, gangs, drug abuse, etc. The youth are our future. Allow God's compassion to flow through you to invest time in prayer, kindness, education, mentoring and whatever else God has assigned you to do to pour into them. They need to know that someone cares for them. We are the ones who exemplify Christ's goodness.

Another gentleman who is vice president of a bank in an impoverished area told his story. He conducted a workshop on budgeting and finances for youth. He talked about saving money and planning for the future. A teenage girl said mockingly, "That's all good what you are saying to us. But none of us will live past 25 years old!" Once again, this was their reality. What she said devastated the executive. For a moment, he was speechless. However, he recovered with words of encouragement, hope and the admonition to set their goals higher than their environment.

For those of us in Christ, it is time to become mature and know that God loves you and you are to love others. There are all types of distractions and road blocks designed to hinder you from your purpose. Stop worrying about your needs. In Philippians 4:19, He said he would supply all of your needs according to His riches in glory by Christ Jesus. Stop worrying about your health. By Jesus Christ wounds (stripes) you are healed (1 Peter 2:24).

Receive it! We have the God (and His kingdom within us) who has already healed us through the blood of Jesus Christ.

Reach out from within you. There is so much in you. God is in you. He works in us both to will and do His good pleasure (Philippians 2:13). Repent right now if you have been off track and get on the path of doing exploits. The Lord has you in the palm of His hand; no one can pluck you out (John 10:28).

Always remember, you can start where you are. There is a saying "each one, reach one." To make someone's day brighter, make a simple gesture of a smile or share inspirational, encouraging words. Be intentional of how you will Be God's conduit of His grace and love. We are ministers of reconciliation. The Word of the Lord says,

> Now then we are ambassadors for Christ, as though God did beseech you by us: we pray you in Christ's stead, that ye be reconciled to God.
>
> 2 Corinthians 5:20

God desires that we are reconciled to Himself. I believe that in the heart of every good estranged father, there is a desire to be reconnected with his children. When we see those who have been rejected by society in pop culture, sometimes it was just one bad decision that landed them in their predicament. Some people have not been hugged nor touched in a humanitarian manner. However, if we operate through God's love they can be rescued and loved. Let's follow this example in the first book of John.

> Beloved, let us love one another: for love is of God; and every one that loveth is born

of God, and knoweth God. He that loveth not knoweth not God; for God is love. In this was manifested the love of God toward us, because that God sent his only begotten Son into the world, that we might live through him. Herein is love, not that we loved God, but that he loved us, and sent his Son to be the propitiation for our sins. Beloved, if God so loved us, we ought also to love one another.

1 John 4:7-12

Sometimes the disheveled outward appearance of individuals may startle some people. Be the one that looks beyond a dirty or disfigured face, missing limbs, or anything that may be deemed undesirable. Always do and speak as the Lord directs you in those situations. These people have situations where they are rejected. On the other hand, there are those who are perceived to "have it all together," with every hair in place, clothing in pristine condition, etc. You might be surprised to know that their life is "jacked up," without God and with no peace. Jesus came and died then arose from the dead to be everyone's wisdom, righteousness, healer, deliverer, savior, sanctifier and redeemer. No one is excluded. So, do not let the outward appearance dictate to you as to how to approach them. A person's eternal soul is at stake. They are in a life or death situation so look past the external to see the eternal.

While we look not at the things which are seen, but at the things which are not seen: for the things which are seen *are* temporal; but the things which are not seen *are* eternal.

2 Corinthians 4:18

One day as I was sitting in my car preparing to go into a fast food restaurant, I noticed a couple of very scantily clad young ladies going inside. They exited a car that had very dark tinted windows. I could not see the driver at all but in my spirit, I sensed that this person was their pimp. For many years, the neighborhood I was in was known to be very popular for sexual solicitation.

My heart went out to those very young ladies. While I was in my car, I said a quick prayer for them. Then the Lord spoke to me saying, "When you approach them, ask them a question." He instructed me to ask them, "Sometimes don't you just want to be free?" After I placed my order, I noticed that the ladies had been in the restroom the entire time. When they exited the restroom, I recognized that one of the girls had been crying. Her eyes were watery and puffy. The other young lady who seemed "more experienced" returned to the car. The other young lady was about to place her order. This was a great opportunity to approach her. I discreetly came near her so that the driver of the car would not recognize that I was talking to her. I asked her the question. She looked at me through tear-stained eyes and said, "Yes." I gave her a tract entitled, "How to Start a New Life." I instructed her to hide the tract and call the church for help ASAP. My prayers are still working for that young lady. I believe in my heart that God set up a divine appointment for us that day.

We are to go out into the world to do His will as the prayer states in Matthew 6, "thy Kingdom come. Thy will be done in earth, as *it is* in heaven." God sees and knows everyone's potential because we are made in His image and after His likeness. He knows each one of us intricately before we made our grand entrance into terra firma. In Psalm 139 that I talked about in the last chapter, verses 13 through 15 in the *New Living Translation* tell us that the Lord watched us as we were knitted together in utter seclusion in our mother's womb. What a mighty and awesome God and Father!

The late great Dr. Martin Luther King, Jr. said, "In a real sense all life is inter-related. All men are caught in an inescapable network of mutuality, tied in a single garment of destiny. Whatever affects one directly, affects all indirectly."[21]

In Luke 14, Jesus shared a parable about a certain man who was hosting a banquet. He invited several people, but all of them had reasons or excuses as to why they could not attend. This displeased the host, and he asked his helper quickly to invite the poor, maimed and blind and to go into the streets compelling them to come to the banquet. This group of new invitees came and participated in the feast.

We are to be the voice, the hands and the feet of our Lord Jesus Christ. There are those who are in the upper echelon of life that need a Savior as well, and Jesus is the answer. No matter our social status, religion, education, age, ethnic background, gender, whether transgender, confused about your gender or whatever—we are here to serve one another. A Russian literary giant, Leo Tolstoy wrote,

"The simplest and shortest ethical precept is to be served as little as possible…and to serve others as much as possible."[22]

God is sending us as light into a dark world.

Everyone is looking for answers. Christ Jesus IS the answer. Start with Him and His light will shine on so many areas where darkness has cloaked and clouded minds, dreams, visions, health and purpose.

If you feel that you cannot make it any further and you have come to the end of your proverbial rope, then you are in an awesome position to look up. This signifies that indeed you could use assistance from the Source, the Lifeline, God the heavenly Father. Surely, there are distractions and hindrances that will present themselves in life. However, focusing on Jesus is key because He is our champion who initiates and completes us. Hebrews 12:2 instructs us to keep our eyes on Jesus. What we observe is what we become. When we firmly fasten our eyes on Jesus, we become more like Him. Keep your eyes on the Word of God (John 1) which is a mirror to evaluate ourselves. Do you see yourself as the Word of God declares you to be? He declared you healed (1 Peter 2:24). You are saved and made righteous according to Romans 2:23. You are prosperous, and your mind is resolute (3 John 2). Consider His Word which shows you exactly who you are (only) in Him. This will help you to be a better expression of God Himself.

> So all of us who have had that veil removed can see and reflect the glory of the Lord. And the Lord—who is the Spirit—makes us more and more like him as we are changed into his glorious image.

> 2 Corinthians 3:18 NLT

A veil covers and conceals things. When a veil is removed, what was once hidden is now revealed. In the kingdom of darkness, sin has people blinded by darkness and groping their way through life and circumstances. However, when Christ is received and the veil is removed, sight is unobstructed, without hindrances and distractions. There is no more shame and there are no more filters that we set up. Filter things only through the Word of God and the blood of Jesus Christ.

Consider the dove bird. The eyes of the dove are created as such to focus on only one object at a time. When our spiritual eyes are focused only on what God is doing in the realm of the Spirit, we will hold fast to the integrity of His Word. What are your eyes focused on?

You may ask, what's in this social responsibility clarion call for me? Don't worry about it. God's Word says in Romans 8:28, "And we know all things work together for good to them that love God, to them who are called according to *his* purpose." When you love the Lord and follow His directions, you will easily give of yourself, your time, and resources knowing that God keeps perfect records of your work. We are also being viewed by (spiritual) witnesses as recorded in Hebrews 12:1–2 NIV.

> Therefore, since we are surrounded by such a great cloud of witnesses, let us throw off everything that hinders and the sin that so easily entangles us. And let us run with perseverance the race marked out for us, fixing our eyes on Jesus, the pioneer and perfecter of faith. For the joy set before him he endured the cross, scorning its shame, and sat down at the right hand of the throne of God.

Chapter Ten

Is Mankind's Will Stronger than God's Love?

Can mankind's will be stronger than God's love? You may wonder is that possible? God does not override a person's will. Have you ever loved someone so much and your pure love kept them alive? Everything living on the earth is temporary. Sometimes an individual has suffered an illness for an extended period of time and their will is to die. Unfortunately, all the love from their loved ones cannot keep them alive.

There is a story about a building project called "The Tower of Babel" in the book of Genesis.

> "And the LORD said, Behold, the people is one, and they have all one language; and this they begin to do: and now nothing will be restrained from them, which they have imagined to do.

Genesis 11:6

The will is the center of a person's mind, which is the CPU or central processing unit as with a computer's motherboard. The mind is where we make decisions and according to Newton's First Law, "our physiological makeup is to follow our most dominant thoughts."

A regenerated spirit is converted to hear and

obey the One who created it. No one is exempt from temptations that are ever present. Paul puts it like this.

> So, I've discovered this truth: Evil is present with me even when I want to do what God's standards say is good. I take pleasure in God's standards in my inner being. However, I see a different standard at work throughout my body. It is at war with the standards my mind sets and tries to take me captive to sin's standards which still exist throughout my body. What a miserable person I am! Who will rescue me from my dying body? I thank God that our Lord Jesus Christ rescues me! So I am obedient to God's standards with my mind, but I am obedient to sin's standards with my corrupt nature.

Romans 7:21–25 GOD'S WORD®

In verse 25, it mentions our corrupt nature has the propensity to sin. Therefore, we must continually make the right choices and then our body will obey. We have the ability to remain and operate in the godlike nature. Conversely, wrong choices can result in people being homeless and hungry, addictions, having their child ensnared in sex trafficking, etc.

Some people are focused on the acts of sin. Even cities have imposed a "sin tax" on cigarettes, alcohol and junk food. Actually, imposing a tax will not stop people from continuing their expensive habits. Cities are taking advantage of people's weaknesses and habits and are using these monetary gains to make a profit or "meet a budget."

Jesus paid for sin in full by sacrificing Himself. The sin of rejecting Jesus Christ consequently sends a person to hell. Its everlasting fire is originally not mankind's portion. Jesus said in Matthew 25:41 that hell is "prepared for the devil and his angels." Once you have accepted Christ, a continuous shift needs to take place to renew your mind to God's Word with a regeneration and a washing of water by the Word (Ephesians 5:26). Therefore, the renewing of our mind is essential according to Romans 12.

> And do not be conformed to this world [any longer with its superficial values and customs, but be transformed and progressively changed [as you mature spiritually] by the renewing of your mind [focusing on godly values and ethical attitudes], so that you may prove [for yourselves] what the will of God is, that which is good and acceptable and perfect [in His plan and purpose for you].
>
> Romans 12:1-2 AMP

Jesus said this in the book of John.

> For God did not send the Son into the world to judge *and* condemn the world [that is, to initiate the final judgment of the world], but that the world might be saved through Him. Whoever believes *and* has decided to trust in Him [as personal Savior and Lord] is not judged [for this one, there is no judgment, no rejection, no condemnation]; but the one who does not believe [and has decided to reject Him as personal Savior and Lord] is judged already [that one has been convicted and sentenced], because he has not believed

and trusted in the name of the [One and] only begotten Son of God [the One who is truly unique, the only One of His kind, the One who alone can save him].

John 3:17–19 AMP

Although some will reject Jesus Christ and His love, eventually all will bow and declare that Jesus Christ is Lord to the glory of God. Even those who are currently bowing, worshipping, and declaring that an idol is their god will have to bow their knee to the only wise God. Their idols could be wood, stone, or otherwise. Everyone will bow! Below are three biblical scriptural references with a message for those who accept and those who reject.

Please note I am unapologetic for these triple references. Since God deemed it important to mention it three times, I am in agreement with His will.

1st Reference

Consult together, argue your case and state your proofs that idol worship pays! Who but God has said that these things concerning Cyrus would come true? What idol ever told you they would happen? For there is no other God but me—a just God and a Savior—no, not one! Let all the world look to me for salvation! For I am God; there is no other. I have sworn by myself, and I will never go back on my word, for it is true—that every knee in all the world shall bow to me, and every tongue shall swear allegiance to my name.

Isaiah 45:21–23 TLB

2nd Reference

For none of us liveth to himself, and no man

dieth to himself. For whether we live, we live unto the Lord; and whether we die, we die unto the Lord: whether we live therefore, or die, we are the Lord's. For to this end Christ both died, and rose, and revived, that he might be Lord both of the dead and living. But why dost thou judge thy brother? or why dost thou set at nought thy brother? for we shall all stand before the judgment seat of Christ. For it is written, As I live, saith the Lord, every knee shall bow to me, and every tongue shall confess to God. So then every one of us shall give account of himself to God.

Romans 14:7–12

3rd Reference

Let this mind be in you, which was also in Christ Jesus: who, being in the form of God, thought it not robbery to be equal with God: but made himself of no reputation, and took upon him the form of a servant, and was made in the likeness of men: and being found in fashion as a man, he humbled himself, and became obedient unto death, even the death of the cross. Wherefore God also hath highly exalted him, and given him a name which is above every name: that at the name of Jesus every knee should bow, of things in heaven, and things in earth, and things under the earth; and that every tongue should confess that Jesus Christ is Lord, to the glory of God the Father.

Philippians 2:5–11

For some this will be a glorious day. The penalty for sin has been paid in full. The gift of salvation is available to all who will believe and accept.

However, some won't believe. On that great day, there will be no excuses.

> Look! He comes with the clouds of heaven. And everyone will see him—even those who pierced him. And all the nations of the world will mourn for him. Yes! Amen!
>
> Revelation 1:7

God is always guiding us through the Holy Spirit according to John 16:13 or drawing us with lovingkindness (Jeremiah 31:3). Every day, there are opportunities for us to make choices. God choices will always produce good success. He promised us,

> This day I call the heavens and the earth as witnesses against you that I have set before you life and death, blessings and curses. Now choose life, so that you and your children may live.
>
> Deuteronomy 30:19 NIV

This is great news! God has given us the free will of choice. He gives us the answer that not only we can live, but our children as well.

Chapter Eleven

Sexuality – God's Plan

And God blessed them, and God said unto them, Be fruitful, and multiply, and replenish the earth, and subdue it: and have dominion over the fish of the sea, and over the fowl of the air, and over every living thing that moveth upon the earth.
Genesis 1:28

God intended for a husband and wife to establish a meaningful marital relationship where children are produced within the union to replenish the earth. If this is not upheld the opportunity for a procreative family is lost. It is understood that sometimes couples are unable to have children naturally. Then adoption, fostering a child or other options are alternatives. Future generations and the opportunity to replenish the earth can also be threatened and cease when individuals choose to identify themselves as a gender other than how they were born.

We have to come back to God's plan for the sexes. When a person's ultimate goal in life is to express their sexuality, then I question who really has their future. Is it God's perfect plan for their future or Satan's deviate plan? Some are confused in regards to their gender, but God is not confused. If there is any confusion, ask yourself what is your Maker's intent or purpose for you being born male or female?

The devil is a master deceiver to bring torment, chaos and deception to the mind. The devil has watched mankind throughout the ages looking for opportunities to steal, kill and destroy (John 10:10). He cannot create, only imitate. His endgame is death and destruction. Imitators are not originators. Imitators actually are thieves because they steal the originator's intellectual property. Satan is out to steal God's creation, us. He is not capable of reproduction to replenish the earth in any manner at all. Satan was formerly called Lucifer before being evicted from God's presence. He was the anointed cherub with the responsibility of being a cover or guard for the Almighty God. He was one of God's most beautiful creations until iniquity (deviance and wickedness) was found in his heart.

> Thou hast been in Eden the garden of God; every precious stone *was* thy covering, the sardius, topaz, and the diamond, the beryl, the onyx, and the jasper, the sapphire, the emerald, and the carbuncle, and gold: the workmanship of thy tabrets and of thy pipes was prepared in thee in the day that thou wast created. Thou *art* the anointed cherub that covereth; and have set thee so: thou wast upon the holy mountain of God; thou hast walked up and down in the midst of the stones of fire. Thou *wast* perfect in thy ways from the day that thou wast created, till iniquity was found in thee. By the multitude of thy merchandise they have filled the midst of thee with violence, and thou hast sinned: therefore I will cast thee as profane out of the mountain of God: and I will destroy thee, O covering cherub, from the midst of the stones of fire.

> Thine heart was lifted up because of thy
> beauty, thou hast corrupted thy wisdom
> by reason of thy brightness: I will cast thee
> to the ground, I will lay thee before kings,
> that they may behold thee.

Ezekiel 28:13–17

Satan's mode of operation and appeal is to our flesh and the lust of our eyes, and the pride of life. His desire is for us to deviate from God's original purpose and get caught up in pride just like he did. We are instructed not to love the world's system (1 John 2:15–17) which is steeped in pride. The Word of God says,

> But if our gospel be hid, it is hid to them that
> are lost: in whom the god of this world hath
> blinded the minds of them which believe
> not, lest the light of the glorious gospel of
> Christ, who is the image of God, should
> shine unto them.

2 Corinthians 4:3–4

Did you notice that god in reference "to the god of this world" is written in the lowercase "g"? This denotes that the god of "this world's system and principles" is Satan. The enemy's goal is to blind a person's mind to what truth in the light of the good news of Jesus Christ is.

Let's look at pride for a moment. The sin of being "lifted up" or pride is what resulted in Lucifer being removed from God's presence. Pride is selfish ambition. It separates us to ourselves and prevents us from having the ability to receive what God has for us, which is customized and perfect. His way of promotion is the "low road" of humility and He will lift us up (James 4:10). Without direction from God, we are like hamsters on life's wheel rapidly going nowhere. The Holy Bible has many scriptures on what God thinks about pride, being proud, a proud look, exalting one's self, etc. It is of a certainty that God does not look nor think favorably toward pride. He does love people but He hates pride (Proverbs 6:16-17). There is a political ideology and social movement in pop culture called Gay pride or the LGBTQ movement. Let that ideology sink in for a moment. For those who are spiritual, what and who do you see behind the movement?

At the beginning of this chapter, I spoke about how the devil wants to destroy us via our sexuality. When people question in their mind who and what they are gender-wise, this sounds similar to the account in the garden of Eden (book of Genesis) where the devil used the serpent to deceive Eve and twisted what God had said. The devil has been around for ages watching God's creation, their tendencies, generational proclivities and what appeals to them. He doesn't give up easily and is a hard task master to his demons (angels) who do his evil work. The same ancient spirits that caused Sodom and Gomorrah to defy God's original intent of marriage between a man and woman as husband and wife are in operation today. They are proudly out of the proverbial closet.

One day, I turned my calendar to reveal the new month's photo. The picture for the month was a beautiful rainbow. In my spirit, I was strongly compelled to revisit the account in Genesis, chapter nine, where God placed the rainbow in the sky as a covenant to Noah that He would not destroy the earth with a flood saying, "neither shall all flesh be cut off any more by the waters of a flood." God is astonishingly amazing! I was elated as I was reminded of how God's covenant is still in effect.

A couple of days later it had rained in my neighborhood. The sky was now clear, and it was a sunny day. As I was driving, I looked into my car's rear view mirror and noticed a rainbow. I quickly pulled into a parking lot and got out of the car so I could get a better view. My sister was with me, and I told her of my recent study of the rainbow in the Bible. We were in awe as we also noticed that it was a double rainbow. Other people pulled into the parking lot and saw the rainbows too. Another young lady pulled over so her children could get a better view of the rainbows. She was approximately 20-23 years old. She asked me, "What is the meaning of a rainbow?" I was glad to respond to her regarding the origin, meaning and significance of the rainbow. I then referred her to the scripture in Genesis, chapter nine. I shared with her how I conducted a recent study in the Bible of the rainbow. As we took pictures of God's glorious rainbows, they began quickly to fade away. Some people seemed unfazed at the beautiful sight, but I know God is always speaking. The question is; are we listening? When I was a child, I was taught the Word of God by mother; therefore, at a very young age, I was familiar with several Bible stories. I hope the mom I spoke with that day teaches her children.

With each passing generation, are we leaving a legacy of God's Word *in* our children? Notice I wrote "in" not "to." Are we making deposits in our future generation or are we just casual and convenient with that responsibility like leaving a

Bible on the coffee table? Are we teaching them the precepts of God? The Word of the Lord tells us in Deuteronomy 6:1–9 to teach His Word to our children.

There is moral decay all around us. I believe it is like a slap in God's face to use God's covenant reminder of a rainbow to be a banner of a prideful display of the abomination of homosexuality. I am sharing with you the pure Word of God and what He says to mankind. He is our Creator and did not make any mistakes when He said, "be fruitful, multiply and replenish the earth." The Holy Bible has several references to how we are to live a life in alignment with that commandment. It is not a suggestion. As I said, there are many biblical references but here are two scriptures that support His stance.

> If a man also lie with mankind, as he lieth with a woman, both of them have committed an abomination: they shall surely be put to death; their blood *shall be* upon them.
>
> Leviticus 20:13

> For this cause God gave them up unto vile affections: for even their women did change the natural use into that which is against nature: and likewise also the men, leaving the natural use of the woman, burned in their lust one toward another; men with men working that which is unseemly, and receiving in themselves that recompense of their error which was meet.
>
> Romans 1:26–27

If you are currently struggling with anything in regards to your sexuality, God can heal and restore you from the inside out. You can live a life free from torment so that your soul may prosper and be whole, not fragmented. Do not allow your soul be a place for disembodied evil spirits that are not advocates for prosperity. Evil spirits are always looking for a place to dwell and hide.

A dry place is where there is no washing of water with the Word of God. Just as the account of Luke, chapter eight, when Jesus Christ cast the demons out of a man, they asked to go into pigs. Allow your body be the temple of the Holy Ghost (1 Corinthians 6:12–20). We have a loving and forgiving God. He will receive you with open arms no matter what you are struggling with. Titus states it perfectly.

> For we ourselves also were sometimes foolish, disobedient, deceived, serving divers lusts and pleasures, living in malice and envy, hateful hateful, *and* hating one another. But after that the kindness and love of God our Saviour toward man appeared, not by works of righteousness which we have done, but according to his mercy he saved us, by the washing of regeneration, and renewing of the Holy Ghost; which he shed on us abundantly through Jesus Christ our Saviour; that being justified by his grace, we should be made heirs according to the hope of eternal life.
>
> Titus 3:3–7

Just as Jesus told Peter, "Satan desires to sift you as wheat," and that He had already prayed for Peter that his faith would not fail and told him when he was converted that he should help his brethren, we are to do the same (Luke 22:31–32). Jesus has prayed for us as well. The Word of God states that Jesus Christ is eternal in the heavens, and He forever lives to intercede or intervene on our behalf (Hebrews 7:25).

Friends, please know this, that the plans and thoughts that God has toward you are only good as Jeremiah writes,

> "For I know the plans I have for you," says the LORD. "They are plans for good and not for disaster, to give you a future and a hope. In those days when you pray, I will listen. If you look for me wholeheartedly, you will find me. I will be found by you," says the LORD. "I will end your captivity and restore your fortunes...."
>
> Jeremiah 29:11–14 NLT

Chapter Twelve

Your Personal Encounter

Whosoever shall confess that Jesus is the Son of God, God dwelleth in him, and he in God. And we have known and believed the love that God hath to us. God is love; and he that dwelleth in love dwelleth in God, and God in him. We love him, because He first loved us.

1 John 4:15–16, 19

Would you like to have an encounter with God's love? If yes, Jesus Christ is available 24/7, 365 days a year. He has been waiting patiently for you. Will you answer the call to salvation?

For salvation that comes from trusting Christ—which is what we Preach—is already within easy reach of each of us; in fact, it is as near as our own hearts and mouths. For if you tell others with your own mouth that Jesus Christ is your Lord and believe in your own heart that God has raised him from the dead, you will be saved. For it is by believing in his heart that a man becomes right with God; and with his mouth he tells others of his faith, confirming his salvation. For the Scriptures tell us that no one who believes in Christ will ever be disappointed. Jew and Gentile are the same in this respect: they all have the same Lord who generously gives his riches to all those who ask him for them. Anyone who calls upon the name of the Lord will be saved.

Romans 10:8–13 TLB

God has designed you to be a success and to prosper physically, financially, relationally, spiritually and psychologically. You can live your best days now!

If you are ready to finally ReCeive all that God has planned for you, say this prayer aloud to invite Jesus Christ to be Lord over your life.

Jesus Christ, I come to you just as I am. You know my life; you know how I have lived. I ask that you forgive me. I repent of my sins. I denounce everything that is against your will and purpose for my life.

I believe in my heart that Jesus Christ died for my sins, arose from the dead and is the Son of the living God. I confess you as Lord and Savior of my life.

I am free from sin and I am full of the righteousness of God only because of the blood of Jesus Christ. Therefore, I am saved in Jesus Christ's Name, Amen. Hallelujah!

Welcome to the royal family of God! From this day forward, live for the Lord and read His Word. Enjoy your relationship with your heavenly Father. He will lead and guide you as you seek Him in all of life's choices. Ask God to lead you to a Holy Bible-believing and teaching ministry so that you stay connected with Him and fellowship with others of like precious faith.

I love you and pray that you realize God's incomparable love daily!

If you would like further assistance in living a life filled with success, my information is listed at the end of this book.

Celeste ❤

Endnotes

[1]*Oxford Dictionaries Online*, s.v. "essence," Def. 1., 2016 *Oxford University Press*, accessed January 8, 2016, https://en.oxforddictionaries.com/definition/essence.

[2]*Bible Hub Online*, s.v. "agape," accessed December 30, 2016, http://biblehub.com/greek/26.htm.

[3]*Bible Hub Online*, s.v. "kosmos," accessed December 30, 2016 http://biblehub.com/greek/2889.htm

[4]Ibid.

[5]*Thesaurus.com*, s.v. "giving," *Roget's 21st Century Thesaurus, Third Edition*. Philip Lief Group 2009, accessed March 8, 2016, http://www.thesaurus.com/browse/giving.

[6]Trimm, Cindy. *PUSH: Persevere Until Success Happens Through Prayer*. Pennsylvania: Destiny Image, 2014.

[7]*Bible Hub Online*, s.v. "agapao," accessed December 30, 2016, http://biblehub.com/greek/25.htm

[8]Ibid.

[9]*Bible Hub Online*, s.v. "elohim," accessed December 30, 2016, http://biblehub.com/hebrew/430.htm

[10]*Hebrew4Christians Online*, s.v. "tev-zayin," accessed December 30, 2016, to avoid irreverently writing the name of God tev-zayin is used as 16 instead of yud-vav as the latter are subsets of God's name, http://www.hebrew4christians.com/Grammar/Unit_Eight/Letters_as_Numbers/letters_as_numbers.html.

[11]Slick, Matt. "What is Biblical Numerology?" *Christian Apologetics and Research Ministry*. (November 22, 2008), accessed December 30, 2016, https://carm.org/what-biblical-numerology.

[12]Ibid.

[13]*TheFreeDictionary.com*, s.v. "re," *Dictionary of Unfamiliar Words* by Diagram Group Copyright © 2008 by Diagram Visual Information Limited, accessed December 30, 2016, http://www.thefreedictionary.com/re.

[14]*WordReference.com*, s.v. "ceive," *Word Reference Random House Learner's Dictionary of American English* © 2016, accessed December 30, 2016, http://www.wordreference.com/definition/-ceive-.

[15]*Bible Hub Online*, s.v. "pater," accessed December 30, 2016, http://biblehub.com/greek/3962.htm.

[16]Ibid.

[17]Ibid.

[18]*Bible Hub Online*, s.v. "azab," accessed December 30, 2016,

http://biblehub.com/greek/3962.htm.

[19]*Bible Study Tools Online*, s.v. "forsake," accessed December 30, 2016, http://www.biblestudytools.com/lexicons/hebrew/kjv/azab.html.

[20]*Dictionary.com*, s.v. "dis," *Dictionary.com Unabridged. Random House, Inc.*, accessed on October 8, 2016, http://www.dictionary.com/browse/dis.

[21]*Goodreads.com Online*, "A Quote by Dr. Martin Luther King, Jr.," *Goodreads*, accessed December 30, 2016, http://www.goodreads.com/quotes/432654-in-a-real-sense-all-life-is-inter-related-all-men.

[22]*Goodreads.com Online*, "A Quote by Leo Tolstoy," *Goodreads*, accessed September 28, 2016, http://bit.ly/2imp8TE.

About the Author

Celeste R. Goff is a gracious, empowering leader who assists people in eradicating fear and building confidence to reveal their internal gifts and maximize their greatest potential. This is accomplished by trusting in the God who created them and getting in alignment with His will for their lives. She has an immense appreciation for life. Father God demonstrates daily His love for her. Therefore, her love for Him is reciprocal with worship and praise. She is a dynamic conference speaker and conducts empowerment workshops. Celeste is a humanitarian involved with several community initiatives.

She is the founder of Epitome of Excellence, NFP a kingdom career development organization that specializes in using tools to help people identify and fulfill their purpose in the marketplace. Celeste is also Principal of Ultimate Business Consulting Plus. For 17 years, she has worked both as a Human Capital and Business Consultant translating businesses' strategic intent into employee tactical plans aligning with organizations' goals and objectives. The optimal result is twofold—engaged employees and excellent business operations. Her clients have included leading corporations such as Tribune Company, Cancer Treatment Centers of America, USG Corporation and Rush University Medical Center.

Celeste has a BA degree in Human Resource Management from DePaul University, Chicago, IL. She is a graduate of the Joseph Business School in Forest Park, IL. She is also a minister graduating from the Kingdom School of Ministry in Atlanta, GA.

Connect With Celeste

/celestegoff

@CelesteGoff

/CelesteRGoff

/celestergoff

Celeste R. Goff

P.O. Box 7672
Westchester, Illinois 60154
email: receive@celestergoff.com

www.celestergoff.com

www.ingramcontent.com/pod-product-compliance
Lightning Source LLC
Chambersburg PA
CBHW062002040426
42447CB00010B/1864